The Eugenic Marriage

Volume III

by

W. Grant Hague

ISBN: 978-1-63923-215-4

Printed: May 2022

Cover Art By: Amit Paul

Published and Distributed By:
Lushena Books
607 Country Club Drive, Unit E
Bensenville, IL 60106
www.lushenabooksinc.com/books

ISBN: 978-1-63923-215-4

The Eugenic Marriage

A Personal Guide to the New Science of Better Living
and Better Babies

By

W. GRANT HAGUE, M. D.

*College of Physicians and Surgeons (Columbia University), New
York; Member of County Medical Society, and of the American
Medical Association*

In Four Volumes

VOLUME III

New York

THE REVIEW OF REVIEWS COMPANY

1916

TABLE OF CONTENTS

CHAPTER XXIV

THE FORMATIVE PERIOD

CHAPTER XXV

HOW TO ACHIEVE

CHAPTER XXVI

SPARE MOMENTS

The study habit—The germ of self-culture—Millions of tiny cells in our brain—The economic value of the study habit—Two[Pg iv] ways of gaining knowledge—Happiness in the company of those striving for higher ideals—A young wife's incentive to self-culture—The difference between moral and mental disloyalty—The study habit creates its own interest—Nosophobia, or the dread of disease—"Keep still and be well" ...

The Home

CHAPTER XXVII

DOMESTIC QUALITIES

A good housekeeper and home-maker—What constitutes a good housekeeper—Preparation and selection of meals—Washing dishes—Pots and pans—Dusting and cleaning—Work cheerfully and be thorough—Don't be a dust chaser—Don't get the anti-sunshine habit—Air your rooms—The ideal home—The medical essentials of a good meal—What makes the home—Working for something—The average housewife's existence is slavery—What shall we work for—Making ends meet—Rest and recreation—Try a nap—Get enough sleep at night—Go out of doors—Take a vacation now and then—Life insurance—Owning a home—The cheerful wife and mother—The indifferent wife and mother—Husband and wife ...

CHAPTER XXVIII

HOW WE CATCH DISEASE

How we catch disease—How germs enter the lungs—How germs work in the body—The function of the white blood cell—How an abscess is formed—The evil habit of spitting in public places—Sunlight and germs—Why it is necessary to open windows—Facts about tuberculosis—The tendency to disease—The best treatment for tuberculosis—Consumption is a preventable and a curable disease—When delay is dangerous—What to eat and wear in hot weather—Scientific dressing—Drink plenty of water—What to drink when traveling ...

Diseases of Women

CHAPTER XXIX

DISEASES OF WOMEN

Diseases of women—The beginning of female disease—Ailing women are inefficient—as home-makers, as wife, as mother—*Few ailing women become pregnant*—The chief cause of female disease—The existence of the average[Pg v] mother—Female diseases are avoidable—The story of the wife—Women who don't want children—Abuse of the procreative function—What the woman with female disease should do—Cancer in women—Cancer of the breast—Cancer of the womb—What every woman should know about cancer—Change of life—The menopause—The climacteric—The average age at which the change of life occurs—Symptoms of the change of life—Importance of a correct diagnosis—Danger signals of the change of life—Conduct during the change of life ...

The Patent Medicine Evil

CHAPTER XXX

THE PATENT MEDICINE EVIL

What mothers should know about the patent medicine evil—Tonics—Used by temperance people because it could "stimulate"—Stomach Bitters—Blood Bitters—Sarsaparilla—Celery Compound—Malt Whisky—Headache remedies—Pain Powders—Anti-headache—Headache Powders—Soothing syrups—Baby Friend—Catarrh powders—Kidney Pills—Expectorant—Cough syrup—Lithia Water—Health, wealth and happiness for a dollar a bottle—New Discovery for Consumption—Consumption Cure—Cancer cures—Pills for Pale People—Elixir of Life ...

CHAPTER XXXI

THE PATENT MEDICINE EVIL (*continued*)

The —— Consumption Cure—Personals to Consumptives—Nature's Creation—Female weakness cures—Various compounds and malt whiskies ...

CHAPTER XXXII

THE PATENT MEDICINE EVIL (*continued*)

How patent medicine firms and quacks dispose of the confidential letters sent to them. Patent medicine concerns and letter brokers—The patent medicine conspiracy against the freedom of the press—How the patent medicine trust crushes honest effort ...

CHAPTER XXXIII

THE PATENT MEDICINE EVIL (*continued*)

The patent medicine evil and the duty of the mothers of the race—"Blood money"—The people must be the reformers—Mothers' resolutions ...

CHAPTER XXIV

"The achievement of an object is dependent upon our determination. Effort is a matter of will. Failure is a product of misdirected determination."

THE FORMATIVE PERIOD

The Best Age at Which to Marry—Incompatibility of Temperament—A Happy Marriage Need Not Be a Successful One—The Evils of Early Marriage—The Wedding Night, its Medical Aspect—The Honeymoon—When Marital Relations are Painful—Times when Marital Relations Should be Suspended—The First Weeks and Months of Wifehood—The Formative Period—A True Marriage—A Wife's True Position in the Household—Only Five Per Cent. of Happy Marriages—Period of Adaptation—Differences of Opinion—Differences of Principle—The Attainment of Success—Arguing Trifles—You Must Know What You Want—The Right Kind of Wife—Contributing to Her Husband's Efficiency—What Are the Requisites of Efficiency—Good Health—Thoroughly Cooked Meals—Rest at Night—Having a System—Enough Exercise—Freedom from Worry—Do Your Part—The First Quarrel—Fault

Finding—The Husband's Efficiency Depends Upon the Wife—
Work Must be Interesting—The Wife's Part.

THE BEST AGE AT WHICH TO MARRY

In order to determine the best age at which to marry, we must be
guided by certain fixed standards. We must find out from
statistics the average age of the parents of the best babies. We
must determine and analyse the qualifications of what constitutes
the "best" babies, according to the eugenic ideal. We should give
heed to the fixity of temperamental characteristics in order to
determine their adaptability to conditions that prevail at certain
ages. We should select an age in advance of the period at which
science has determined individuals to have outlived any
hereditary tendencies.

We have abundant proof that the best babies are born of parents
between the twenty-third and the twenty-sixth[Pg 332] years. We
know also that the age which responds, with the fullest degree of
plasticity, to temperamental characteristics, is in the early
twenties. We know, likewise, that inherited tendencies may be
said to have been outlived at or about the twenty-second year.
The ideal marrying age, therefore, is, for both male and female,
approximately the twenty-third year.

The physical, mental and moral development of both men and
women, at this period, evidence a high degree of adaptability,
and are responsive to the institution of marriage. Their hereditary
traits, if any previously existed, assume a dormant form at this
age. They have cultivated the temperamental qualities which
they will retain, with few modifications, throughout life. On the
other hand, their dispositions are responsive to reason, and are
capable of readjustment. Their temperamental characteristics are
plastic, and under favorable conditions it is possible for both to
evidence a degree of sympathy and toleration that bespeaks
future harmony and success. No marriage can result in mutual
happiness and success if one of the participants is
temperamentally incapable of changing his or her convictions.
One of the fundamental essentials to peace in the home is the
quality of adaptation to circumstances, and no other virtue will
be called into existence oftener than this quality. At this age, a
man is eager to contribute to the contentment and happiness of
his partner, even if it is necessary to sacrifice his own whims and

opinions, and a woman, at this period, is temperamentally so constituted that she will respond to the same impulses.

Incompatibility of temperament simply implies that two individuals are so constituted that they cannot, or will not, adapt themselves to the temperamental characteristics of each other. This condition is one of the most prolific causes of unfortunate marriages. Age has a great deal to do with this situation. Men over thirty have unconsciously developed habits of judgment and are too set in their opinions and ways to accommodate themselves easily, or without friction, to the temperamental differences that will undoubtedly exist in their wives. The spirit of adaptation, which is a characteristic of[Pg 333] younger years, is lacking, and a mental readjustment is scarcely to be expected. We, therefore, frequently observe in the marriage relations of certain individuals a spirit of friendship existing rather than that of companionship which should be the quality that binds them together. Statistics prove that "affinities" creep into the lives of those who marry early, or in those who marry after thirty. This form of domestic infelicity may be rightly regarded as a product of "incompatibility of temperament."

A happy marriage need not be a successful one. Some couples attain happiness through sorrow, grief, and failure. The so-called happy marriage, like happiness itself, is only a myth, made up of anticipation and memory. You have only to look into the calm and wrinkled faces of old women, and talk to them to discover that the outcome of unselfishness and abnegation forms the nearest approach to happiness in married life or out of it. It is the bearing of the burdens of life that constitutes its happiness.

The Evils of Early Marriage.—No woman has the vitality to stand the strain of maternity before the twenty-third year. If a girl marries at eighteen years of age she gives the world children totally unfit to struggle with its problems. At about twenty-two years she may give one child of value to the world, but all others following will be increasingly unfit. In early marriages children are apt to come too frequently, and this is one cause of infant mortality. Statistics show that children born with an interval between them of only one year have a mortality of one hundred per cent, higher rating than those born with an interval of two years. And if these children are the progeny of very young mothers the percentage is even greater. The percentage of children who are malformed and idiotic is greater among those born of too young parents. It has been shown that the child can only inherit what the parents possess. If the parents are not of an age when all the powers are at their highest, the child is robbed of just this amount of growth and force lacking; no amount of education or training can supply this loss.[Pg 334]

There is another feature of early marriages that should receive serious consideration. A girl of eighteen or twenty has not reached that period of growth where certain inherited tendencies will show. If she has inherited a predisposition to consumption she may outgrow this period provided she is permitted to reach her full growth without subjecting her constitution to any strenuous physical or mental strain. If, however, this girl marries and becomes a mother, the incident effect upon her health will most likely weaken her to the extent of bringing to the surface the inherited tendency. Many mothers succumb to just such conditions, where had they remained single until a later period they could have assumed the responsibility of maternity without any evil consequences.

The idea that by an early marriage a woman can train and change the inborn characteristics of her husband is a mistake. Few women can reform a husband after marriage. If she cannot reform him before marriage she will never do it afterward. These inborn traits will have their way despite anything she may be able to do to change them—only the man himself can control and govern them. During the period of this temperamental transformation the function of parenthood should not be exercised. Only when a man's character is fully matured should he be permitted to transfer it to another generation.

The idea has been advanced that early marriages will tend to preserve youth from sowing wild oats. The woman who is the victim of this delusion will reap a harvest of discontent and misery. Any man who needs the sacrifice of a woman to cultivate the art of self-control is not a fit citizen, far less a fit husband or father. A man who is willing to bring children into the world before he is a self-governed animal does not understand the first principles of race-regeneration, and it is the duty of parents to educate their sons and daughters in this fundamental idea. To be an efficient parent one must be mentally, morally, and physically developed.

The Wedding Night;—Its Medical Aspect.—The fundamental object of true marriage is the propagation[Pg 335] of the species. Woman plays the more important part in the consummation of this duty inasmuch as she is the origin and depository of the future being. It is, therefore, most important that she should not be wholly ignorant of the nature and responsibilities of her position. Suffering, disease and death may result as a consequence of ignorance of these matters. It is the duty and the privilege of medical science to state, in language which all may understand, the facts regarding this interesting human event.

It would seem as though suffering to some degree, characterized each epoch in a woman's life; menstruation, marriage and maternity. Much may be done, however, to lessen the pain necessary to the consummation of marriage. Not infrequently difficulty is experienced in this respect and great care, forbearance and gentleness must be exercised or unnecessary pain and injury may result. It is quite possible to cause serious injury by unrestrained impetuosity and this must be guarded against. It is sometimes absolutely necessary to consult a physician, especially in cases where greater resistance is experienced than is to be expected. These are rare cases.

The first conjugal approaches are usually accompanied by a slight bleeding. They may not be so, however, and the absence of blood has no significance or meaning. The most suitable time to select for marriage is midway between the monthly periods. This is a season of sterility, and as the first nuptial relations may be followed by indisposition, pain and nervous irritability, it would be well to select a time when these ailments shall have an opportunity to subside before the appearance of the disturbances incident to pregnancy.

The Honeymoon.—From a medical standpoint there is great need of a radical change in the way in which this nuptial period is spent. For many weeks previous to marriage the bride's existence is a long drawn-out period of nervous tension. Instead of enjoying mental and physical rest and repose, every moment of the time is crowded with exacting incidents, which, ordinarily, would wreck the nervous system of a robust individual. If this exciting preparatory experience ended in a period of rest[Pg 336] and recuperation, it might not prove physically disastrous, instead of which, however, we know that the bride is subjected to a series of physiological tragedies which few weather with impunity. At no time of her life is she more in need of being surrounded with all the comforts of home and the intelligent direction of sympathizing friends who understand and appreciate the crisis through which she is passing. Custom, however, dictates that she shall be hurried from place to place at a time when the bodily quiet and the mental calmness and serenity so desirable to her should be the only object in view.

Marital relations still continue painful and will be so for a few weeks. Too frequent indulgence at this period is a fruitful source of various inflammatory diseases, and often occasions temporary sterility and ill health. In many cases constitutional disturbances and nervous disorders have their beginning at this time and these unfortunate conditions are directly caused by the discomforts incident to the silliness of the social custom which deprives the woman of the rest and quiet necessary.

The awakening of the sexual function is a tremendously important medical incident in the life of any woman. The simplest mind may adequately understand why such an experience should be consummated in a cheerful environment of domestic comfort and peace. To drag a girl around sight-seeing, when her nerves are on edge and supersensitive; when she is physically unfit, weary and not at all interested; when her brain is apprehensively busy with secret conjectures in which her husband even may not participate, is a species of torture which the average bride submits to with the best grace possible because social custom dictates the stupid programme.

Mothers should approach this subject with tact and diplomacy, but they should, nevertheless, approach it with firm intentions to persuade their daughters to consider the situation from a common sense standpoint. The custom of the honeymoon survives because young brides do not appreciate the facts involved. It is the mother's duty to acquaint them with the truth, and no sensible mother will plan, or agree to a honeymoon that involves continuous discomfort and possible serious consequences[Pg 337] to the health of her daughter at the beginning of what should be the happiest period of her life.

When Marital Relations Are Painful.—Nature did not intend that the act by which the earth is to be replenished should be painful. If therefore, pain is a constant characteristic of this function, it is an evidence that disease exists and it should be given attention at the earliest possible moment. A displaced, congested womb is most frequently the cause. Such displacements most likely are a result of imprudence in dress, constipation and general negligence on the part of the victim. To delay or postpone assistance in such cases is dangerous, while on the other hand, relief is prompt and as a rule satisfactory if taken in time.

Times When Marital Relations Should be Suspended.—There are times when such relations are eminently improper. There are certain legitimate causes for denial by the wife.

Intoxication in the husband is a good reason for refusal. Idiots and epileptics have been produced as a result of one parent being intoxicated when fecundation took place. Many cases are on record whose history is well authenticated where the mental faculties of the offspring have been totally destroyed.

Convalescence from a severe sickness is a just cause for sexual abstinence. The existence of any local or constitutional disease which would be aggravated by marital relationship is also a just cause of refusal. The existence of a contagious disease renders a refusal valid. Sexual intercourse should never be permitted during the menses. Pregnancy is unquestionably a just cause for refraining from all marriage duties.

The First Weeks and Months of Wifehood.—The daughter is established in her own home: she is now the young wife, the prospective mother. What can we say that will be helpful at this period—those wonderful first weeks and months of wifehood? Her guiding star will unquestionably be the unconscious lessons she has absorbed from the tactful talks with mother. She will unwittingly pattern her conduct, to a large extent, after her, and follow the routine mother adopted in the old[Pg 338] home. But there is a new factor to be considered. Her life, present and future, her possibilities, her very happiness, is dependent upon the husband. The old saying, that, "you must live with a man to really know him," she will find to be all too true. The story of her future life might be safely told if we could know how she will meet the new vicissitudes. She has known her husband only as a sweetheart, she has clothed him with virtues that exist only in her imagination, will he measure up to her expectations? She is watchful and tactful,—the little mother-talks she remembers. She did not believe when mother told her, that he had qualities which she would only find out after marriage, but she knows now. She is learning that household duties are exacting and fretful; that, though married, life still has a few thorns. She finds out also that the long day, when husband is at business, affords many opportunities for reflection and serious thought. These moments of seeming leisure are the moments of destiny. They are the introspective moments, when she weighs and measures out for herself sympathy, if she is not made of the right stuff, or she makes strong resolutions, and prepares herself mentally to win out in the new life. They are the moments when her subconscious intelligence is trying to express itself in the spirit of truth and honesty, when she weighs and measures and analyses the exigencies of the new environment. Her destiny depends upon the inspiration that is impressed upon her brain as a result of these self-communings.

Most of us would not follow exactly the path we trod had we the opportunity to live our lives over again. The young wife has the chance to "do it over again." She has the opportunity of a new beginning. She should regard this opportunity as the most precious gift she will ever obtain. Many would give untold wealth for her chance. Happiness and riches lie at her feet. All the experiences that make life worth living are within her grasp. It all depends upon herself. An enthusiast is apt to be insistent. If his cause is just we gain by his insistency and determination. We are enthusiasts on this subject, we want you to believe in our disinterested sincerity.[Pg 339] We believe,—in fact we know, that the first few months after marriage is the critical period in every woman's life so far as the attainment of happiness and success is concerned. No physician can practice medicine for years and fail to have this truth impressed upon him again and again.

Every intelligent person knows that most young girls enter into the marriage relationship without a real understanding of its true meaning, or even a serious thought regarding its duties or its responsibilities. Maternity is thrust upon these physically and mentally immature young wives, and they assume the principal role in a relationship that is onerous and exacting. We know that the duties of wife and mother require an intelligence which is rendered efficient only by experience. We know that young wives acquire habits which undermine their health and their morals unwittingly. And we also know that the product of this diversified inefficiency is what constitutes the decadence and the degeneracy of the human race. Is it any wonder that mistakes occur, that heartaches abound, and that homes are degraded?

What is the remedy? Education! Systematized instruction; an efficient and everlasting propaganda of education carried into the homes of the thousands of young wives and mothers who are willing, but who do not know how to play their part creditably and efficiently.

The Formative Period.—The period prior to marriage is the formative period, the character building years. Matrimony is to be the test of how we have built our castle. The success of the matrimonial venture—for every marriage is an experiment—depends absolutely upon the result of the first year. We would, therefore, seriously, and earnestly, request the young wife to think deeply upon this problem and not to ignore the fact that the success of the venture is absolutely dependent upon her efforts to a very large degree. Some may assert that the husband is the essential equation, so far as happiness and success is concerned in the matrimonial venture. We do not think so. A home is what the woman makes it. A man may not be an ideal husband, or even a good father, though his home, to his children, may be heaven[Pg 340] itself if the wife is a born mother and a good woman. On the other hand a man may be patient, hard working, self-sacrificing, good father, but he cannot make a happy home, for his children, if his wife is not the right kind of a woman.

A true marriage implies love and confidence, and in the vast majority of marriages these qualities can be regarded as tangible, and may be used as any other business equity is used, for a certain time. The length of time depends upon the use to which this asset is put during the early months of marriage. It is the utilization of this time, how best to employ it, that concerns us here.

A word as to a wife's true position in the household may be opportune. There is no question but that her status has changed in the last generation. Whether this change is for the better is a matter of opinion. It is too large and too intricate a problem to be fully discussed in a book of this character. Any opinion on such a subject must of necessity, in our judgment, be a warped one. There are few, very few, absolutely happy and congenial homes. It has been estimated that only five per cent. of all marriages are successful. If five per cent. make a success of marriage why could not the other ninety-five? The reasons are not fundamental or serious—they are trivial as a rule. It is making the right beginning that counts. If this is the secret, and every married person of experience will testify to this truth, the young wife should give the matter her serious consideration. In the life history of every couple there is a period of adaptation, which is sooner or later passed through at the expense of one or the other, or both, resigning themselves to an acceptance of the stronger, or positive, elements in the other's disposition.

Differences of Opinion.—If a woman discovers, for example, that her husband has very decided views upon certain matters, and these views do not in any way conflict with the law, moral or otherwise, and the adoption of them does not necessitate the denial of a principle, it would be far better for her to acquiesce in these views, rather than to obstinately adhere to her opinions,— especially if she cannot, in a friendly way, offer an argument[Pg 341] strong enough to convince him he is wrong. One or the other of every married pair will have to be willing to give in, in all trivial matters that come up from day to day, if a harmonious degree of existence is to be reached.

It is certainly natural to assume that ordinarily the wife will be the one to concede most. She is supposed to be endowed with all the gentler attributes. Therefore our advice,—irrespective of all the arguments which may be made, and which we need not even hint at, here, but which are at the tongue's end of every so-called advanced woman,—is for the young wife to gratefully concede a great deal to her husband.

If a man's daily life is clean, and if his ambition is to work in order to provide a comfortable home for his wife and children, he is deserving of the love and confidence of any true woman. And inasmuch as you have chosen this man for your husband, for your guide and for the father of your unborn children, it behooves you to find out how you may quickly accommodate yourself to be his helpmate, his friend, his confidant and companion, throughout all the years of your life. Let us assure you without fear of contradiction, that you will endear yourself to him by your willingness to be advised and guided by him. Such an attitude will engender a tangible confidence that may be drawn upon to weather temperamental contests that might otherwise prove to be serious obstacles in building up a mutual respect and trust and which is essential to peace and happiness. He will look for your word of cheer, and he will willingly tell you more and more of his inmost thoughts and ambitions, and unconsciously he will rely upon your judgment, your womanly intuition, your help, in every move he makes. The time when you will have to "give in" will have passed away. You will have made yourself part of his life, his mentality, you will have reached the goal of domestic happiness, and that is as near paradise as most of us reach in this world. It all depends upon "how you go about it" in the first few months of married life.

Consider the other picture. If a wife cultivates, or has the inherited inclination to argue trifles, to bicker[Pg 342] over mere matters of opinion, even if she wins occasionally, what does she gain? Nothing! The husband resents the tendency to argument. His pride is wounded at the thought that his wife needs to be convinced of every opinion he advances. Such an attitude completely breaks down the tangible confidence that is essential to peace and happiness. Soon he begins to keep his opinion to himself; the serpent enters the home; the wife finds he is interested in things of which he does not inform her. Jealousy, lack of confidence, doubt,—the skeletons of all domestic peace and happiness soon accomplish their terrible and tragic work, and the end is not difficult to imagine.

Most of the things regarding which husbands and wives quarrel are of no special moment. They are not momentous subjects,—it is usually a trifle that mars the domestic peace. It takes but a few years for most women to appreciate that many of the things that cause heartaches are not of any consequence at all. They originate, as a rule, in one or the other failing to appreciate that the other has certain individual rights which demand some degree of respectful consideration. The ego element in human nature is responsible for a very considerable portion of the domestic infelicity that mars the home life of a large proportion of the people.

Trivial Differences.—Many homes have been broken or rendered permanently wretched by trivial differences. The husband may like to play games, the wife may want to read. One may like to go out to parties and theaters, the other may want to stay at home. Before marriage these differences appear to merest trifles and are the subjects of good-humored bantering; after marriage they cause constant dissension, constant friction. A trifle is the usual beginning, a divorce may be the end. A little lack of tact, an unwillingness to sacrifice self in a small measure "at the right moment" and friction would have ended.

It is a reflection upon our intelligence, and it is rather significant that it should be the little, trifling things that cause most of the troubles and heartaches in the world. We rarely quarrel over the important episodes[Pg 343] Of life; the real things, the things that constitute the measure of our manhood and womanhood. Ask any of your friends, be they Jew or Gentile, Catholic or Protestant, Baptist or Episcopalian, Democrat or Republican, whether, in their best judgment, it is better to be honest or dishonest, clean or dirty, false or true, intelligent or ignorant, an idler or a worker; whether it is better to be gentle and kind or brutal and cruel, a gossip and scandal monger or to mind our own business and to speak kindly of our fellow-man, whether, in short, it is better to be good or bad? And yet these are the real, the fundamental qualities that brand a man, or a woman, or a race of people, as worthy and true and Christ-like.

To the eugenist, a thought obtrudes itself at this point. It is the logical, the link between the cause and the effect. Why do we waste so much time arguing and fighting over non-essentials? Why is the world such a big quarreling-pot over nothing? And the eugenist suggests, if it is not possible, that the explanation may be found, in the fact, that the human family, as a race, is below par; that so many of us are incomplete; that it is the product of the combined mental effort of the unworthy element that makes all the trouble? It is scarcely logical to assume, that an individual who has been brought into the world by healthy, worthy parents, and whose ancestry for generations have been clean, honest people; and whose upbringing and education has been adequate to fit him to become a respectable, decent citizen, could, or would be a trouble maker. On the other hand, can we expect, or are we justified in hoping that an individual whose ancestral record is bad, whose environmental conditions are faulty, whose education has been neglected, who is in all probability physically and mentally deficient, will be capable of conforming to the standards of the other individual? From an imperfect whole, may we not naturally expect bad parts? From a diseased body and mind, may we not look for a low standard of thought and action? And may not these conditions account for the greater part of the little, as as the big, troubles that mar the peace and progress[Pg 344] of the race? Will not the elimination of the eugenically unworthy rid the world of its heartaches and sorrows? It is not only a suggestive thought, it is an inspiration for the exercise of the supreme intelligence of the statesman, the sociologist, the teacher and the preacher alike.

Differences of Principle.—There are more serious differences than those of taste, however. There are differences of principle.

They do not reveal themselves before the promise "for better or for worse." The sentimental days of courtship did not bring them out. But now that they have settled down to the routine of ordinary living, nature brings them to the surface and the issue must be met. It is discovered that the wife is a devout Christian and a faithful church attendant while the husband insists on his wife spending Sunday in the country, or at the seashore. The woman tries to get her husband to go to church but she fails. He tried to get her to accompany him but he does not succeed. There is a rift in the lute, little sorrowful heart pangs on the part of the woman, and the man feels sore and grouchy and wanders away alone, then finally open quarrels and indifference. Two lives are pulling apart. Someone must give in; but which one? The observance of her religious duties to the wife is a matter of principle. The husband's method of spending Sunday is simply habit. He has no right to interfere with her liberty in this respect. The one to give in is the one whose conscience is not trampled upon. If the husband refuses to go to church with his wife, he can do so amicably, and in such a tactful way that his wife cannot reasonably feel permanently offended, but he must not object to his wife going to church, nor has he the right to insist on being accompanied in his outing by his wife. On the other hand, the wife must not nag or quarrel with him continuously on the subject of religion. Those little incidents will come up in the experience of every married couple. They are not serious or insurmountable in themselves, but they can be made serious by mismanagement.

The true wife is the home-maker, not simply the housekeeper. She is responsible for its attractiveness and its[Pg 345] comfort, its morals and its existence. The marriage vow "does not make a wife, but comradeship in the bearing of the burdens of life, does." She must be Love and Justice and Truth to her children, and companion and friend and helpmeet to her husband.

We, therefore, advise the young wife to begin wedded life with definite plans and ideals.

The Attainment of Success.—In the first place, you do want your particular matrimonial venture to be a success. Success in one sense is getting what you want. You must, however, know exactly what you want. Very few people know what they want, but those few are the ones who manage to "get there." If you ask a dozen of your friends what their plan of life is, what they are working for, what they really want, not one of them probably could tell you with any degree of exactness. Most people go along in an indefinite way, working from day to day, more or less dissatisfied, and with absolutely no feeling of certainty as to what the future holds in store for them.

Human effort is an example of energy misdirected and it is the greatest potential energy in the universe. Really to want something means that we must be willing to sacrifice everything necessary to attain our wish, and to concentrate and direct all our efforts in its attainment. To do this, we must be efficient, we must be healthy, we must strive day and night, and we must want intensely to achieve success.

During the first few weeks of married life the young wife, if she is a wise little lady, will take stock. She will begin to think, and she will naturally speculate about the future. She will try to determine the facts in her particular life that are the important ones so far as the attainment of success is concerned. Her material success of course is dependent upon the efficiency of her husband. Now, a married man's efficiency depends almost entirely on his wife. If a man attains great material success, he will acknowledge, if he acknowledges the truth, that his wife is deserving of most of the credit. The husbands of most good, sensible wives are successful. If a man is, unfortunately, married to a woman[Pg 346] who is not a helpmeet, who is not a well-balanced wife and mother, and achieves success, he does so by reason of his innate strength of character and in spite of the unjust drain on his efficiency. Most men under these circumstances however lose heart and interest and become failures.

The young wife, therefore, will definitely plan in just what way she can contribute to her husband's efficiency.

What Are the Requisites of Efficiency? Good Health.—He must have regular meals. The food must be carefully selected and suitable to his personal needs according to the character of the work in which he is engaged. The food must be properly and thoroughly cooked. If he does not understand the science of eating, the wife must educate him. Remember his success means your success, his failure, your failure. If you were in charge of a highly complicated machine, you would not allow it to be ruined by careless misuse. You may have married a healthy animal, but animals are tricky and uncertain. He is still your lover and he will do anything reasonable for you, if you "go about it in the right spirit and in the right way." Be sure you "go about it in the right way." Be tactful, be patient, don't nag. Don't tell him of his faults, simply note them then determine what you want to accomplish. In a little while, he will become enthusiastic and will be telling his friends how to eat, and what to eat, and, later, he may try to convince you that he thought of the idea first. This is the typical man. You will learn how to manage him, and your first success will encourage you—he will be a child in your hands—if you only "go about it right." And this applies to everything you do that has any relation to domestic peace and happiness and final success.

The woman who grasps the meaning of the following truism and determines to practice it, is well on her way to happiness and success. "It is the man that has a system in both life and business that wins the battles." The struggle of life has become so strenuous that most everyone's nerves are always near the explosive point,—the man who has a system in life has discovered that there is[Pg 347] nothing to be gained by being disrespectful or discourteous, or by butting rough-shod into the affairs or interests of other people; tact, diplomacy, flattery, the temperamental capacity to wiggle around the explosive corners of other peoples' irascible nerves to gain your point, is "having a system," and it wins battles. The young wife who knows how to do this, is so far ahead of the army of ordinary young wives, that she need not take time to look around to see if the others are gaining ground. They will never overtake her.

Rest and Sleep.—The husband must get enough rest each night, so don't drag him away to parties and balls and late suppers. Be a philanthropist—give him the care you would give a thoroughbred horse with which you hoped to win a big stake. Let him think, however, that you are doing it for his sake. To you the prize is a greater stake—it means life's failure or success. Remember you are in this fight to win. The gratification of whims and fancies during the first year of married life leads to the establishment of expensive habits, and may be the one factor that will mean failure in the future, when you will wish, with all your heart that you had begun differently. The time to sacrifice, to work hard, to plan ahead, is when one is young; when hope is strong and health is good—not when ambition falters, when age grows weary, when efficiency is impossible, and when regrets crowd in on us and failure crushes energy and hope and happiness. The struggle of life is a real one to every soul born, but it is worth the fight, and the glory of a fight won is the greatest human satisfaction this side of the grave. Try it, try to win.

Enough Exercise.—Be sure your husband is getting enough exercise. If his work is desk work, think out some plan to compel him to take the exercise every healthy animal requires. Make up your mind definitely what is necessary and exactly what it is you want him to do, and then begin to work in your own successful way with that object in view. It may be systematized gymnastic work he needs. If so, suggest to him the advisability of becoming a member of a club or gymnasium, or get two sets of exercisers and begin work on them[Pg 348] yourself if necessary. Devote ten minutes every morning and night to exercise. He will soon follow you, and many happy contests you will have and profitable ones too. Working together is the secret of domestic peace. Even if this reads like slavery or self-immolation, what do you care? You are happy, you are working for something, the time will come when you will have realized your ambition. Domestic happiness and material success are worth all we are asked to pay for them and they are never obtainable on the bargain counter.

It may be outdoor exercise he needs, try golf, swimming, baseball, tennis, anything to gain your point; and, all the time, remember you are leading him by your apron-string because you have discovered the secret of "how to go about it."

Freedom From Worry.—A man cannot work efficiently and worry at the same time. Modern business methods are conducted on such a strenuous basis that, to keep "in the ring," a man needs every ounce of reserve he can command. Don't imagine your husband is totally free from cares and responsibilities just because he is not at business. He may have left his office a few minutes earlier than usual to get away from trouble. Encourage the system. When a man feels in his heart that there is one person in the world to whom he can always turn, and be sure of a loving, sympathetic greeting, one who understands and believes in him, one place he can always go and feel certain of enjoying peace, and comfort and contentment, there is little danger of any friend supplanting the wife, or any club or saloon taking the place of home.

Do Your Part.—The moment you know your husband is in the house, change the expression on your face, smile, even if it pains you, and go to him with a familiar word of greeting and give him a kiss. Do this every day of your life, unless when you are sick in bed, when he will go to you. Establish this habit, and if ever the day comes when he returns from work and there is no greeting, no kiss, stop the whole domestic ship, regard it as a tragedy. Don't let the first entering wedge of discord come into your life. If there is no first quarrel, there will never be a second. If you are at fault you had better[Pg 349] right matters at once or take the consequences. Take our advice. Don't experiment with a man. Deep down, every man is a brute. There is a certain elemental devil in every male animal. Don't rouse it. You are only a woman. Don't invite a quarrel. You will get the worst of it. Keep on the peaceful side of the street. It is always a mistake to talk too much. Words are poison when silence is golden. You cannot make a mistake by leaving the husband alone if he is at fault. Time is a wonderful physician; she will heal almost any wound. Your tact, your silence, your seeming fear (in other words, your method "of going about it in the right spirit and in the right way"), and an opportunity to think it over, will make him ashamed of himself. He will want to crawl back into your good graces and the lesson will be a long remembered one to him,—if, and this is tremendously important—the wife does not glory in her triumph and nag him about it. The temptation to err is great and there are few young wives who can resist it. Keep silent, however. Don't refer to it and you will win more than you know. Blessed is she who can forget what is not worth remembering.

You will have averted the first quarrel and, inasmuch as the "first quarrel" is an historic event in every married woman's experience, it may be worthy of a little further consideration.

The First Quarrel.—Some women become weak in a crisis and spoil their own chances of success, despite the fact that circumstances may have been working in their favor. Some women meet a crisis bravely and do exactly the right thing at the right time but falter and fail after the crisis has passed. Take, for example, the incident we have just narrated. When a husband brings into the home a sample of his real self, for the first time, it is not really an unexpected event, though it may be an unpleasant shock to the young wife; and she must not render it an important incident by mismanagement. Nevertheless, it is in itself a momentous occasion, and it may prove to be the moment of destiny. The spirit of the lover has been the dominant spirit so far, the atmosphere of the honeymoon has continued, there has been[Pg 350] no friction, no quarrel. To-night the husband has carried a business *grouch* into the home, his militant impulses are just below the surface, the slightest unfortunate word, the least lack of tact, a failure to "sense" the situation correctly, will explode the mine and wreck a dream. Deep down in the man's heart he does not want a quarrel but the brute in him will fight if the environment invites it. It takes two to quarrel. Silence on the part of the wife, therefore, is the only solution of the problem. If the first quarrel never takes place the second will never have to be dreaded. Silence, no matter what the provocation may be; no matter how acute the sense of injustice may be, silence is the only safe way out. The husband if left alone, will be ashamed of the situation his lack of self-control has created, the lover spirit will conquer the brute. He will regret the pain he has caused; he will want to forget and be forgiven quickly though he may not go through the formality of an apology. A formal apology and reconciliation will, in his judgment, dignify the episode and make a mountain out of a molehill. The wife will be wise to so regard it though it is an injustice to her. The husband will not underestimate the importance of the event, however, and in many ways will be a better husband in future, but he does not want to talk about it or be talked to regarding it. This is part of the psychology of the male, and the successful wife discovers it early and acts accordingly.

Having safely piloted your craft through the troubled waters, don't prove weak and silly when you reach a safe harbor. When the moment of passive reconciliation arrives, when it is necessary to resume the domestic routine, don't show the spirit of resentment. Be pleasant, don't cry, don't become hysterical. Be strong, ignore the whole affair, leave it in the hands of time and forget it. The victory is yours, don't lose it.

Fault Finding.—At a later date, when, in all probability, the wife will be the one whose conduct will incite trouble because of the worries incident to her more or less monotonous, domestic existence, much care will have to be exercised so that an unwitting fretfulness may not cause quarrels. When a man comes home at[Pg 351] night tired and hungry, longing for peace, and comfort, and pleasant conversation, it is worse than anarchy to not only get no greeting, but to note the discontent on his wife's face, and to listen to a tirade of fault finding. Your husband has troubles of his own. The maid's impudence, the crossness of the baby, the noise of the neighbor's children, the toughness of the meat from the butcher, do not interest him. He is hungry, he wants to eat, and above all, he wants rest and peace. We are considering this subject from the economic standpoint. The young wife must recognize that if she is a fault finder, if she worries her husband, she interferes with his efficiency and jeopardizes the attainment of success,—her own success. From a purely selfish standpoint, it is a bad investment.

It may interest many young wives to know, that a number of large corporations have recently begun to systematically investigate the domestic environment of their employees. If it is found that they are not happy, or that they do not enjoy a restful and congenial home life, they discharge them. They claim that a man who is worried cannot be efficient, and if he is not efficient he is not a dependable individual to have in their employ. Some railroads will not allow an engineer to drive a passenger train after it is discovered that he is unhappily married. The young wife should, therefore, appreciate that she may be directly responsible for her husband's efficiency and success. If a woman is guilty of conduct that interferes with the earning capacity of her husband she is erecting an obstacle to happiness and success that is fundamental, permanent and insurmountable. In justice to herself and to her husband and to the future she should promptly decide if the conditions are such that a change is impossible, and if so she should, in order to avert a tragedy, seek a separation.

Work Must Be Interesting.—No man can exert the highest degree of efficiency if he is not interested in his work. This has become a business truism. How can the wife aid in this matter? By coöperation, by tactful advice, by suggesting new methods, by originating new ideas that may open the way to new possibilities.[Pg 352]

Even menial work is interesting if we regard it as a stepping-stone to something better. It must be done thoroughly, however, to justify this hope. Life is a struggle, a struggle in which many are vanquished and few survive. Only those few survive who fit most perfectly to their environment. If a man is getting proper nourishment and sufficient exercise, and is free from worry, if in other words he has vitality, he cannot possibly fail to give full value for what he receives. His work will at least be satisfactory. If his lack of interest in his work is because it does not fully satisfy his ambition, this is a splendid opportunity for the tactful and resourceful wife.

It was suggested to an enterprising little wife, whose husband was earning a small salary as a bookkeeper, to advise him to study stenography and correspondence at the Y. M. C. A. He did so, and is now the private secretary of the president of a large corporation, at a salary of six thousand dollars per year. His wife encouraged and cajoled him during the long winter nights when he studied late. She sacrificed herself by giving up all social entertainments and other pleasures. She catered to his tastes and comfort, and she talked so entertainingly during spare moments of what the future would be when he was a great success, that he was simply compelled to make good. She got her reward, and the very struggle and effort strengthened their characters, broadened their sympathies, and taught them the true meaning of love and affection.

Other young wives may achieve similar success if they "go about it right." That is the secret. That was the secret of this young wife's success. She first knew what she wanted, she then prepared the way by tactfully showing her husband how he could increase his efficiency. She kept the subject diplomatically before him by directly praising him, assuring him that he had the ability, that he would find it easy, that he was meant for "higher things." Then she drew word pictures of where they would live, the kind of house she would like and the new furniture she would buy, and where they would spend their vacations when he was earning the[Pg 353] salary which she knew he was worth. They began to live in this future, it became part of their life, his pride was awakened, he would be ashamed to fail, he was whipped to the post and spurred to the finish and he won the race, because he had married the right kind of a woman. "The right kind of a woman,"—the woman who knows that "the marriage vow" does not make a wife, but that comradeship in the bearing of the burdens of life does.

The Wife's Part.—Having read the preceding pages some young wives may ask if that is really what being married means? If it is all work and sacrifice and no pleasure? That is exactly what it means and if there is no pleasure in work and sacrifice, then there is no pleasure in married life. The young wife who fails to see the significance of this interpretation of what has been written has a fundamentally wrong idea of what married life means.

A woman who begins her wedded life with less loyal ideals than are depicted in the performance of the duties we have enumerated is imposing on her husband and is false to herself. She will not attain happiness and success. To marry in order to have a good time should be a state's prison offence.

Happiness and contentment and success are products of duty well done. They are the logical recompense for effort and sacrifice. Individual happiness is not the chief object of existence in this life. To work efficiently is the supreme obligation. It is naturally to desire happiness and to labor for it; but it is absurd to be annoyed and angry because we do not find it. Happiness through marriage is never attained except by never-ending self-abnegation and effort.

We must struggle or we will degenerate. A correct interpretation of racial progress proves this truth. Effort is the supreme law. All good things have been given to man at the price of labor.

[Pg 355]

ADVICE TO YOUNG WIVES

[Pg 357]

CHAPTER XXV

"Being forced to work, and forced to do your best, will breed in you temperance, self-control, diligence, strength of will, content, and a hundred virtues which the idle will never know."

Charles Kingsley.

HOW TO ACHIEVE

What the Young Wife Owes to Herself—Why Was I Born—What Are the Personal Qualities Necessary to Success—What Are the Personal Qualities Necessary to Happiness—Self-control—What is a Thought—The Evil Habit of Hasty Judgment—The Bad Thought Habit—Training the Mind—Go About it in the Right Way—Be Sure Your Husband's Friends

Are Your Friends—Be a Good Fellow—Two Kinds of People in the World—Everything Depends Upon What We Do With Our Mind—The Most Popular Woman—The Gift of Flattery—Choosing Your Friends—True Friendship Expects and Demands Nothing—True Friendship is Necessary—"By Your Friends Shall Ye Be Known"—Making Resolves—The Formula of Success—When Fortune Knocks.

What the Young Wife Owes to Herself.—If the young wife is making a conscientious effort to do her duty, there are certain things she owes to herself, to her husband, to her unborn children. She too must preserve her health, her efficiency. In guarding the health and contributing to the efficiency of her husband, she will have done much in this direction. She will, however, have many spare moments at her disposal. We have already remarked that these are the moments of destiny. In the coming years she will look back upon these moments with real pride, or regret, according to how she spent, or misspent them. Let us begin all over again, with renewed interest and enthusiasm, and try to understand just what is meant by this.

Every human being asks himself, or herself, at some time in life, the questions, "Why was I born? For what purpose was I created and put upon this earth? Is there any real object or purpose in living, except to pass the time from day to day, and year to year?" To most,[Pg 358] the reply is perplexing,—and not at all satisfactory. All great minds who have deeply studied this problem, unanimously agree that there is a purpose in life. We are not a thing apart,—an isolated entity. We are part of the living whole; every thought, every deed, every spoken word, every sentiment, every passion, every prayer, is inter-related with every other thought, deed, word, sentiment, passion and prayer of every other living thing in all eternity. We have an ideal to maintain, and if we are untrue or fail, we interrupt, we desecrate the everlasting scheme of the universe. We will therefore be held responsible for our manner of living,—for the sum total of our existence. We have a purpose to fulfill, a responsibility to sustain. If we are false to that purpose, and fail in our responsibilities, we rob the world of the help we should bestow, and, in a far larger measure, we deprive ourselves of benefits and pleasures, every moment of our lives, greater than we can conceive.

The world is many centuries old, and many millions of human beings have lived and died during that time. A certain percentage of these men and women lived lives which bettered the world. They left a thought which will live through all the ages. They proved the truth of some basic unchanging principle. They drew the attention of mankind to the reality of a certain immutable fact. These truths, these principles, these facts, have all been tested, and they have been found to be everlasting. In other words, we find there are certain truths, certain principles, certain facts, that every living thing must obey, must subscribe to, must live up to or perish. Every thought, every deed, every movement, of every living thing, is regulated by unalterable laws which govern our lives and to which we must conform or pay the penalty in failure. Human nature is God's riddle!

What are the Personal Qualities That Experience has Shown to be Necessary in the Attainment of Happiness and Success?—Experience has taught us that certain personal qualifications are essential to the attainment of success and happiness. We must, for example, be master of ourselves. We must have acquired the art of self-control. Self-control is an evidence of a high[Pg 359] intelligence. There are many gradations of mental progress before complete self-control is reached. Complete self-mastery in matrimonial conflicts is a long and difficult acquisition. Probably it is fully acquired in the fewest possible cases. The one who acquires self-control, who gives in during the adaptative period of which we have written, is not the weaker. The young wife should always keep in mind that the underlying principle to be vigorously adhered to in the home, is justice. There will arise many occasions that will severely test your disposition and your patience, but, if you have yourself well in hand, if you understand yourself, you will emerge from the conflict successfully and as a consequence a little stronger. When we acquire the determination to efface self in these domestic squabbles we begin the building of a character.

What is a Thought?—The greatest product of creative inspiration is the human brain. The very fact that each human being possesses one of these marvelous products implies responsibility, the responsibility of what we will do with it. A thought is a creation of brain or mind activity. It may be a bad or evil thought or it may be a good thought. Let us now go back to the young wife just as she is about to begin the hour or so of recreation in the afternoon. Her work being done for the time, let us suppose she elects to do a little fancy needle work. She finds a comfortable seat and is soon apparently engrossed in her work. Is she? Doubtless she is, and a very commendable, harmless, inviting picture she presents, but a thousand thoughts are passing through her mind. It is not the sewing that she does, that will be weighed in the balance, it is not the patient stitch, stitch, stitch, that she takes, that will mark the hour well spent. It is the one thought that will predominate over all the others, that will tell the ultimate tale, because of its effect on her own mind. A thought once created, even if it is never expressed, is as much a created entity as a deed executed.

Suppose this young wife attended a social gathering in some friend's house the evening before, and for some trifling reason she formed an unfavorable impression of[Pg 360] another lady guest; during the hour of her sewing, which we are discussing, she goes over in her mind all the incidents of the gathering, and because of the previous impression, she still thinks unkindly of the lady in question. She passes judgment upon her in her own mind. What has she really done? She has created a thought an opinion, which now becomes a part of her mind, because it is recorded in her brain cells forever, and, inasmuch as she was not justified in passing judgment upon a person's character in this hasty way, she harmed herself by establishing a bad habit,—a habit of hasty judgment,—which will have an effect on her method of judgment as long as she lives. The evil effect may not end here,—it seldom does. A chance remark,—still the product of the hasty opinion,—made to some other woman regarding this lady, will give this other woman an unfavorable impression of the person, and if you could trace all the little gradations of the first unjust opinion, through all the stages of a gossiping community, you would be astonished at the growth, and the evil accomplished by the thought, born amidst the apparently innocent and commendable surroundings of an hour's sewing. If you educate your mind to create bad thoughts you will become a victim of the habit. Each bad thought makes the creation of another bad thought more easy, because a bad habit is, as we all know, a difficult thing to live down. Therefore a bad thought unexpressed does harm only to the individual who creates the thought. If the bad thought is expressed to another party, it is impossible to tell or estimate the harm it may do. Life is what we make it. If we get into the habit of thinking unjust, unkind, selfish, bad thoughts, we live in that atmosphere. Your whole life will be a reflection of your mental attitude. If you feed your mind on such food how can you hope to grow into a contented, happy woman? Let us not dwell upon the dark side. There is another picture, one more inviting, more difficult to realize, it is true, but more perfect as a consequence.

Training the Mind.—There never was a time in the history of the world when so many people were striving after definite knowledge,—some scheme of mentality,[Pg 361] some mental atmosphere,—some spiritual or idealistic phenomena,—which would satisfy the craving, the hunger of the restless and dissatisfied human mind for absolute enlightenment regarding the mysteries of life. It is a curious fact that to attain such knowledge, all these various bodies, no matter how they may differ as to the method of procedure, concede that the education of the human mind and the recognition of its exact capabilities is the ultimate province through which final enlightenment must come.

We must, therefore, recognize that on whatever we do with our mind, in our own little way, will depend the measure of success and happiness to which we may aspire. Success is not attained without effort, but every little effort we expend will help wonderfully in the task. Train your mind to think just, kind, good thoughts. Do not dwell upon the bad side of any problem, search for the good side, because every problem has a good side. So also has every human soul. When the unkind, the unjust, the bad thought is conveyed to you by another, do not admit it, do not dwell upon it, render it negative at once by assuring yourself that there is another side to the question. We all know how easy it is to kick the under dog. We all have in mind some friend, some acquaintance, some old lady, perhaps, who is famous in her community for her kindly ways, and for her kindly thoughts. The two go together. It is well known among her friends that she will not tolerate any unkind, unjust, evil report, of even the humblest or lowest member of society to be expressed in her presence, without instantly defending the maligned victim, by picturing the possible other side. Her life has been an example, an inspiration in the community, because she has always exerted a kindly, sympathetic, helpful influence. It is this atmosphere, this environment, that checks gossip, stifles scandal, saves heartaches, and prevents domestic tragedies.

The most interesting study you will ever engage in, if you are true to yourself, will be the working of your own mind.

The resourcefulness of your brain will be a constant[Pg 362] pleasure to you. You will be aided by books and you will find a lesson in every thing you see and hear. Life will appear different, and you will rise above the plane in which the little routine annoyances of daily life seem burdens and sorrows. A woman, if she goes about it "in the right way," can do with her lover-husband what she pleases. If she uses that power for selfish motives, or for a wrong purpose, in the end she will be the loser. If she is far seeing, and uses her power to build up a home, and is just, and respects her husband, and honestly gives him his true place in her scheme, and loves and honors him, and is tactful, there is no limit to what she may accomplish, so far as the personal happiness of herself and husband and children are concerned. We all know that law is not always justice. We likewise know that there is no such anomaly as a perfect human being. The ability to gain a point, without apparent coercion, or a sacrifice of truth or honor, depends upon the successful qualities that go toward the building up of a complete and harmonious personality. It is an axiom in psychology that to attain the highest success, one must first understand, and, understanding, conquer the bad, and develop the good features in one's own temperament, before attempting to rule the conduct of any other person. You must understand yourself before you attempt to understand your husband. Many of his best qualities,—qualities that if rightly understood, will go a long way toward making your life a happy one,—can be misunderstood, misinterpreted, and become incessant factors for doubt, jealousy and quarreling.

Because your husband prefers to do a thing in a way that does not quite satisfy your taste, does not necessarily mean that he is wrong, and such a condition does not justify an argument. Consider the matter seriously, in silence argue it out with yourself and give his side the same justice you hope to get. If you can develop convincing proofs, that his way is not the best way, even though it isn't really wrong ethically, he will probably concede the point, provided,—and don't overlook this,—you "go about it in the right way, and in the right spirit." It isn't likely you will be given a patient hearing,[Pg 363] if in the past you have been in the habit of nagging and browbeating him. Don't look upon tactful ways of gaining your point as evidence of weakness. It is distinctly an evidence of strength of character, and, each time you win a point in a friendly debate with your husband, you will have gained much. He will respect you all the more because of your justice; and will secretly admire you because of your ability to protect yourself. You will gain confidence in your judgment, and you will see things in a broader, and from a less selfish standpoint.

Your Husband's Friends Should be Your Friends.—Be sure your husband's friends are your friends. Business or professional exigencies do not always permit a man to choose or select his acquaintances. You can be sure, however, he will not ask or expect you to associate with any doubtful person, though it may be necessary to extend a welcome to an undesirable business, or professional associate, for the time being. When these occasions occur, do not mar the opportunity to help by any exhibition of temper, or dissatisfaction. He may be trying to make the best of an unfortunate incident. Help him. Do not discourage him for at heart his object is to gain some business advantage that will redound to your advantage as well as his own.

Nothing pleases a man more than to know that his wife is "a good fellow," that no matter what seems to be questionable on the surface, he can rely upon her to know that everything is right underneath,—that his motive is good.

Do not invite him to tell a lie in order to avoid a scolding. Nothing is more unfortunate, nothing is more easy for an ordinarily good, but misunderstood man, than the tendency to fib about little things, if he feels in his heart that his wife will scold,—that she will fail to see the point. It wounds his self-respect to have to do so, yet he selects the minor evil as he sees it, he sacrifices his manhood in the interests of domestic peace.

Two Kinds of People in the World.—Roughly, there are two kinds of individuals in the world, the individual who will, and the individual who will not. There are[Pg 364] individuals who will not see the truth, who fail to see the point in an argument, who are obtuse and obstinate. This trait is largely wilful perversity and ignorance. We cannot help noting them in the passing, but we scarcely hope to interest them, though we cannot restrain our sympathy.

Young wives who come within this category will remain the laggards, the degenerates. Their evolution is revolution, they become the fault-finders, the discontents, the gossips. They do not love themselves nor are they loved by any human being. They are the domestic failures. As wives they dishonor the sex, as mothers they dishonor God.

In reality, there is but one thing in the universe—mind. By "mind," we mean the ability to reason. Every human being comes into the world with this ability. Our health, happiness, efficiency, success, depends absolutely upon how we utilize this birthright. There is no limitation to this ability. Heredity and environment have little to do with it. It is a personal equation. "It depends upon how you do it," has been frequently reiterated in the preceding pages. This implies, to what use you put your mind, and this is the secret of the young wife's efficiency and success. True happiness is a mind product. It is a creation of mind activity. The evanescent pleasures are not character builders, but a created thought is a pregnant possibility. The young wife who begins her wedded life with ideals with the determination to succeed, with certain well thought out plans, will progress. Her world is her husband and her home. Her husband must succeed, her home must be comfortable and happy. She must contribute her full share in achieving these results. If she permits her personal amusement to be the dominant purpose she will fail. She cannot transgress the law and remain immune. How can she begin right? Give her best to her home. A woman who gives her most gracious smiles and her most captivating manners to society, is false to her husband and her home. The prettiest gown and the brightest jewels should grace her own dinner table. To bring them out only to attend a reception, or a tea party,[Pg 365] is a desecration. Many women expend their moral and spiritual strength upon the "club," and bring the withering remnants as a sacrifice to the blighted home fireside. We have no right to help build a church, or foster a philanthropy by depleting our strength and resources in the effort, only to give the frazzled ends of our talents to home and home-making. Nor has a woman any right to exhaust her strength in the toil of mere housekeeping, and reserve for the evening hour of conversation a bundle of quivering nerves and an exasperated temper. These women are not home-makers. Their ideal of wifehood and motherhood is fundamentally wrong. Every power of the body, and of the mind and spirit, should be devoted to the achievement of a home atmosphere. It is the creation of this quality that spells contentment, peace, happiness, and no other.

A young wife with an ideal, with a definite plan, and with a true appreciation of her dignity and importance, will never find time to daily gossip over the back fence with her neighbor, nor will she join the sewing circle whose function is well known to be scandal bartering. "Give your best to your home,"—one of the great advantages of having a specific plan is that it wholly engages our mind. If we have an object in view, if we want something, it implies interest, and if we are interested deeply in something we think about it. Every spare moment will be used by the mind in devising ways and means to achieve our purpose. We will not find time to seek the questionable amusement of gossip. The women who are eternally poking their noses into other people's business, who burden their minds with other people's affairs, who are busybodies, always neglect their homes and their children. They have no ideals, they are the derelicts of the community. Remember that "Satan finds some mischief still for idle minds to do."

The Most Popular Woman.—The most popular woman is the one whom a majority of all women would vote for in a popularity contest. Many women are so notoriously vixenish and jealous of members of their own sex, that, it would seem to be worth while to analyze the qualifications of the most popular woman, in an effort[Pg 366] to discover the one quality which appeals to her own sex. After exhausting the list, we find the most popular woman possesses, in a high degree, the quality of tactful, or diplomatic flattery. The art of flattery is an acquired habit. Statesmen and politicians know its value. Even the little seekers after public office cultivate it assiduously. It is undoubtedly an asset of much value in every sphere of life, but it must not be overdone. Every member of the human-family will tolerate a large amount of it without showing resentment. This is the reason why it is a valuable asset and of such general usefulness. Sometimes a woman will boast that she detests flattery, yet she is highly pleased when you tell her that the one quality you admire in her is that she cannot be flattered. If, therefore, the young wife desires to become popular, for her own sake, or if she regards this as one way to contribute to her husband's efficiency, should his success depend upon public approval,—she may cultivate the art of diplomatic flattery. The cultivation of any art is not a one-sided accomplishment. It is beneficial in many ways, and aids distinctly in character building. No one, for example, can acquire the art of tactful flattery and retain a sour or mean disposition. To flatter efficiently you must seem delighted, and the delight must express itself in smiles and kindly words. These habits will impress themselves upon your inner consciousness, and before you know it, the habit will be a constituent part of your temperamental armamentarium.

The most popular woman will acquire the habit of making some flattering observation every time anyone's name is mentioned, and she will never be guilty of criticising a living person or a dead one. She will make it her rule in life, in order to sustain her reputation, never to make an enemy. She will cultivate the insinuating art of shaking hands, of smiling sweetly, and of making apropos remarks. No one will ever leave her without feeling that she is an exceedingly gracious person. She will even convey to them, in her inimitable way, the impression that she thinks they are "just right." She will use "blarney" as a science in an artful way.[Pg 367] The flattering remarks she will make regarding others will be passed along by those to whom she makes them, and she will be responsible for an epidemic of egoism all over town. It is a wonderful art.

If the young wife keeps this up for some time she will begin to notice certain things. She will be accorded much flattering attention herself and she will be treated with marked consideration wherever she goes. She will be received cordially, and every aspiring other woman will make strenuous efforts to include her among her friends. She will be invited to participate in public functions when members of her sex take part, and she will be favored and her interests furthered in all social organizations.

She will, without doubt, wear her laurels becomingly, and her success will be easily acquired. Her spirits, and her health will promptly respond to the elixir of her interesting labors. Life will be full of new and surprising interests and it will be well worth the effort expended. Sleep will be more refreshing, she will not be troubled with nerves, and her appetite will be a source of profound thankfulness to her. She will radiate a quality of good-fellowship that will be infectious, and her whole philosophy of existence will be charity itself. Surely it is worth while.

Choosing Your Friends.—The young wife should choose her friends with caution. Remember you are beginning a new life in which even trivial matters may exercise an influence that will be bad. One should appreciate the difference between true friendship and indulging in friendly relationship with promiscuous acquaintances. A physician has a better opportunity of observing the conduct of the feminine element of a community than any other person. We have come to divide young wives into two types: those who attend strictly to their own affairs, and those who mostly attend to their neighbors' affairs. It is not too much to say that a young wife's time will be wholly occupied if she has begun her housekeeping career with the intention of becoming a home-maker. She cannot, therefore, afford to waste her time with promiscuous acquaintances.[Pg 368] Women who become promiscuous in their friendships have time to waste for a number of reasons,—

1st. Their husband and home is not their whole existence. If success and happiness depend upon how the first year of wedded life is employed, then husband and home should be the young wife's whole existence.

2nd. Women with time to waste have no ideals. Women without ideals are not home-makers. A home-maker cannot acquire any information from a woman who wastes her time in idleness.

3rd. Idleness creates mischief. One who is idle is a mischief maker. An idle brain is looking for amusement, and as the impulses of an idle brain are evil, these women are gossips, and scandal-mongers, and home-breakers.

4th. True friendship demands nothing. Promiscuous friendship on the other hand does demand something, and as these women live in the evil atmosphere, they live mentally on scandal and gossip. This is their mental plane and they give and take nothing higher than that which they understand.

The young wife will, therefore, be wary of this form of friendship. Infinite harm is being done in every community in the country in this way. No home, no person is too sacred for the vituperative tongues of these scandal-mongers. They are densely ignorant though they may be fluent talkers. They ingratiate themselves into the confidence of a willing victim, learn the victim's secrets, and rend her to pieces on the next street corner. Many a man has begun wedded life with the laudable intention of helping to mold his young wife's mentality, of preserving her innocence and purity of thought, only to be undone by the evil machinations of these human derelicts. He will be amazed and astonished at the opinions she gives utterance to, and if he does not find out where she is getting them, and check the desecration going on, she will be beyond his reach in the very near future. No self-respecting woman will tolerate such acquaintances. There are, however, many innocent, pure women, who are innately too gentle to assert themselves by insulting another woman at this stage of their experience,[Pg 369] who have the makings of a good wife and mother, who wittingly become victims by reason of their very gentleness, and consequently lose their ideals, and drift into failures.

True friendship is necessary. Many men and women rightly attribute their whole success and happiness to having had the right kind of a friend or friends. Charles Kingsley when asked by Mrs. Browning to tell her the secret of his life, said, "I had a friend," A friendship that is not an inspiration, an incentive to higher thoughts and nobler deeds, is not true. "True friendship demands nothing." It gives. We should cultivate the friendship of those who know more than we do, so that we may learn and profit by the relationship. Some people radiate sympathy and helpfulness and inspiration. Instinctively we can tell those people when we come into their presence. We leave them, not once, but always, with the feeling that there is something about them that energizes and inspires. They draw out our better selves. We are conscious of our shortcomings and faults, and in their company we strive to give utterance to worthy thoughts. We feel capable of great deeds. If we could surround ourselves with these friends, we feel that life would mean more, and that we could accomplish much. "He that walketh with wise men shall be wise." This is where true friendship is valuable. These moments of inspiration help us to pull ourselves together. We climb a little higher; we see further and clearer; we learn the meaning of life's duty; they change the whole complexion of living. The little things, the annoyances, the disappointments, the failures, the pains, the sorrows, the passions, we see in their true perspective and they no longer usurp importance, because we are beginning to learn the significance of the things beyond. The incidents of life are no longer life itself.

One friend, one true friend to the young wife, will indeed be a tower of strength to her. Every young wife needs a friend. The desire for sympathy dwells in every human heart. Even the assiduous person needs encouragement and a little praise. It is wonderful how a mite of laudation will prod us to be more worthy. Even[Pg 370] our joys never intoxicate save in the telling. By sharing our happiness and joys with another we double them. True friendship means confidence, affection, harmony, love. To be in harmony with one person means that we invite the harmony of all mankind.

If man is made in the image of God every human being must be more or less divine. Confidence, affection, harmony, love,—the attributes of true friendship,—are the divine sparks in our humanity. True friendship, therefore, is growth in the divine sense. There are real things in life which we seldom acknowledge but which are, nevertheless, real. We do not often admit the existence of the divine in ourselves, but it is there. If we did acknowledge it oftener we would live nearer the truth, nearer God.

When we read in the public press the story of the *Titanic* disaster, how after all the boats had gone, and the ill-fated ship poised, before she took her awful plunge, how the doomed souls stood on her decks and lifted their trembling voices in unison with the brave orchestra to the strain of "Nearer My God to Thee,"—something clutches at our heartstrings, and we find the divine reality trying to come to the surface to express itself in that universal friendship out of which heroes are made. When we stand by the bedside, watching the fitful, final breaths of a well-loved child, or of an old, honored and faithful mother, there creeps into our consciousness feelings with which we are strangers, but they are ours, part of the divinity in us which in the work-a-day-world we stifle and crush. Friendship and no other human quality brings this divine element into our actual life. Those who have never had a friend have never solved the riddle of human nature.

We must remember, however, that there are those whose lives are denials of this divinity. They are incapable of true friendship, and they, in prosperous days, deride the sentiment involved and consider any reference to such matters as silly and mawkish. These blustering heroes, however, are the ones who shriek the loudest when fate places them on sinking decks.

Strive to be worthy of a true friendship. Be willing to give of the best that is in you. We need the inspiration of the divine that is hidden in us, we should not crush or fail to acknowledge the presence of the still, small voice that speaks of love and for love. Remember, that, "By your friends shall ye be known."

EXPLANATION OF SYMBOLS

Used in the Following Three Illustrations

HEREDITARY FEEBLE-MINDEDNESS[A]

The above chart illustrates the first great law of hereditary feeble-mindedness; that if both parents are blighted all offsprings will be blighted. The family represented is plainly very low grade. It is one of that kind found in every community, growing like rank weeds to menace society. It is small wonder that with production like this permitted criminality springs full-fledged into the world.

This chart is particularly interesting, showing as it does the marriage of a normal man with, first a normal woman, and subsequently with feeble-minded women. The taint of the feeble mind is inevitable. Whereas the grandchildren by his second marriage appear normal there is always the danger of their progeny being blighted by the taint that is in their blood. The horror of the third marriage is too evident.

[A] "Feeble-mindedness; Its Causes and Consequences," Goddard, The Macmillan Company.

[Pg 371]

Making Resolves.—In a preceding chapter I remarked, that every human thought, deed, act, prayer, etc., must conform to certain laws, if by their use we desired to achieve results. We know this is true, but we do not always obey the rule, and in the end we wonder why we are failures.

Psychology has formulated laws, based upon actual experiment, regulating every department of mental endeavor, or every branch of systematized mental achievement. These laws show that there are fixed rules, by which mental effort is regulated, systematized and classified, and that the human mind conforms to these laws even when working in ignorance of them. No matter how we may deduce facts, or reason from analogy, we obey fundamental principles.

In a recent magazine article I read the following:

"This is my own story of why and how I rose, fell and rose again. It would not be told but for the fact that I have learned by an Experience mixed with some bitterness, that all such things are governed by fixed business laws and rules and move always in obedience to them. There is as I know, a law of failure and a law of success. There is even a law of mediocrity. Every man is controlled by that one of these three laws which he elects to invoke and to follow."

"The laws themselves are fixed and unchanging; man is the only variable unit in the equation. He succeeds, he fails or he slumps into mediocrity according to the law with which he voluntarily or by predisposition puts himself in harmony. This is my belief, based on my own adventures with these laws and my observation of other men who have dined and lived with them on intimate, though not always friendly, terms."

This was written by a successful business man in an article reviewing the "ups and downs" of his business experiences. It does one good to read such confessions. To the thinking individual it suggests the need of serious, whole-souled, conscientious effort. If these laws exist,—as they most certainly do,—what is the use of trying to[Pg 372] achieve results in a wrong way? Why not conform to these laws and concentrate our effort in the right direction? A prodigious amount of energy is wasted in efforts to beat the game. One may scheme and contrive until all ambition withers and hope fades, but no one will ever find a satisfactory substitute for hard work. Many lives have been frittered away in the foolish attempt to find the "easy road." It is doing the little things of life conscientiously that counts. The humble hen does one thing well. She lays eggs to the extent of three hundred million dollars per year, in this country alone. If we combine her egg yield with her chicken industry we find her harvest yields the enormous sum of six hundred and twenty million dollars per year.

We are precisely what we deserve to be: we fit for what we are fitted for. Weaklings are sent to the rear, fighters are always in front.

The young wife may resolve to win; it depends upon how she begins to mold herself for larger possibilities. If she cannot succeed in small things she will not fit when the task is bigger. Suppose you resolve to be considerate and agreeable to every soul you meet for one month. For one month you will subject yourself to a rigid test, you will be considerate and agreeable, no matter what the conditions are or the provocation may be to break your word.

It is a fact that most failures are directly attributable to laziness rather than to lack of ability or poor health, or any other cause. It is the most difficult thing in the world for some people to exert themselves to "make the effort" to succeed. They just do enough to "hold their job" or to earn a living, though the possibilities around them are rich in promise. Many know what they ought to do, but they don't seem to be able to do it. Their ambition is lacking; they elect to travel the road to failure.

If the young wife resolves to be considerate and agreeable for one month, she is the right kind of young wife. The right impulse is working within her. The very fact that she makes the resolve proves this. Most people are influenced by two motives, necessity and pleasure. They[Pg 373] work because they have to work to exist. But a great deal of the work is indifferently done. The woman who skims over her household duties in a disinterested and frequently slovenly way, will spend much thought and a great amount of time to excel in appearance and in attaining results at a church fair, for example; or she will work assiduously sewing every afternoon and evening on dresses, etc., to shine during a two weeks' vacation at the sea shore, while her husband is being indifferently fed and her home all but neglected. To attain pleasure one will actually work efficiently though the method and the motive may be ethically wrong. So, when a young wife actually resolves to do something which has a high moral significance and which she is not compelled to do she is being actuated by the right kind of principle, she is following the law or instinct of success.

The Formula of Success.—Successful men and women are frequently asked to give their formula of success. There is no formula of success except hard work. Every successful man or woman is a hard worker. There is no exception to this rule. We often personally know of men or women who "rise in the world" and sometimes we look upon them as lucky dogs, and wonder why fortune does not favor us. If we analyze the daily life of these seemingly lucky individuals we will find that they plan and work and scheme while you and I play and amuse ourselves. They have a certain system which they adhere to under all circumstances. They have worked hard so long that it has become a habit,—a habit that brings happiness and success. All of them have had their ups and downs, their worries and battles, but they have faced them in the front ranks, they have never become discouraged, they have been inspired and impelled by the conviction that some day the tide of battle would change. On that day they were determined to be ready and willing to take advantage of the turn of the wheel of fortune.

Study the work of the next successful man or woman you meet, and see if the rule does not hold true. It isn't the kind of energy that is generated that makes the distinction between success and failure: it is the way in[Pg 374] which the energy is used. To win means concentration of energy; let the energy be dissipated over many things and failure becomes a certainty. There isn't a really successful man or woman in existence who does not deserve success, and who has not worked hard for it.

Success, fame, and the efforts of friends may not give us the happiness which we yearn for, but there is one thing that will always steer us safely into port—one thing that will bring us the blessing of happiness though all things else fail us—and that is hard work.

When Fortune Knocks.—Fortune is said to knock at the door of every man once in a lifetime. That once is all the time, for the truth is that fortune is knocking at our doors every day. The trouble is that we are not prepared to take advantage of her importuning habits. Fortune has her laws, and we cannot enter her chariot except by obeying these laws. The young wife who resolves to be considerate and agreeable for one month is obeying one of her laws, because, if she keeps her promise, she will have learnt more than she ever did in any preceding month of her experience. She will find, for example, that people are really more amiable and agreeable than she ever thought they were; that, because of the restraint she is exerting on her temper and self-control, she is growing stronger temperamentally. She has more patience, and she is more thorough in little things; her environment is enlarging and life is more interesting. The month's experience will teach her something of her own capabilities and resources, and she will be so interested and encouraged that she will determine to experiment more and in other directions. She is experiencing the psychology of character building—the most fascinating study of that most fascinating riddle, human nature. Fortune always favors the brave—it will favor her because she is working in the right direction—she is obeying the law of success.

To resolve is to obey—to know what you want, to desire to succeed, to be willing to sacrifice self, to attain results, to smile at adversity, to be patient, truthful, honest, unselfish, sympathetic, in short to work hard every minute and all the time.

[Pg 375]

CHAPTER XXVI

"Habit is a cable: we weave a thread of it each day, and it becomes so strong we cannot break it."

Horace Mann.

SPARE MOMENTS

The Study Habit—The Germ of Self-culture—Millions of Tiny Cells in Our Brain—The Economic Value of the Study Habit—Two Ways of Gaining Knowledge—Happiness in the Company of Those Striving for Higher Ideals—A Young Wife's Incentive to Self-culture—The Difference Between Moral and Mental Disloyalty—The Study Habit Creates Its Own Interest—Nosophobia, or the Dread of Disease—Keep Still and Be Well.

The Study Habit.—Every individual differs from every other individual according to his habits. The nature of our habits fixes our status in the struggle of life. If we get into the habit of thinking evil thoughts, we live in that atmosphere. Health is a habit, so also is success. Honesty, virtue, vice, procrastination, contentment, fault-finding, grumbling, candy eating, gossiping, drinking, sleeping, religion, friends, life itself, are habits. Life is what we make it. "As the man thinketh in his heart, so he is." Some habits are good, others are bad. Certain habits are constructive, others are destructive. If we get into the habit of doing our work thoroughly and regularly, according to some definite system, we encourage the habits of contentment, calmness, efficiency, and happiness. If we do our work spasmodically, irregularly, without system, if we gossip between times, we are eternally trying to catch up, so we encourage the habits of procrastination, discontent, inefficiency, fault-finding, and failure. We must be master or victim of our habits. We must succeed, or we must fail. The immutable law of life permits of no standing still. We are either progressing or we are retrogressing. One of the best habits, if not the very best, that the young wife[Pg 376] can cultivate in her new home is the study habit. It is eminently a constructive habit.

The germ of self-culture is latent in every healthy mind. It is an exceedingly virile microbe. It may begin as a fad but intrinsically it grows as a virtue. Environment may give it birth but its roots may not be circumscribed. They seek nourishment from every far and near spring and well, and its branches spread out to the north and south, and east and west, and its leaves suck into its heart, health and strength and color and fragrance, from the everlasting sun.

In our brain are millions of tiny cells. Each cell is capable of a single thought. When we begin as children, we learn letters first, then words, then sentences or thoughts. In due time we have a sufficient number of cells, each with its photographed letter or word or thought. From this stock we reason and think and plan. These are the letters and words and thoughts of ordinary life. We have millions of cells left, and the brain is a tireless, ceaseless worker. If we keep on feeding it more letters, more words, more thoughts, it is satisfied, but if we stop, if we stagnate, it keeps on working, but it can only use the words and thoughts we have given it. Ceaselessly it rearranges these words in its effort to live. We are feeding it nothing, its circulation becomes poor, its vitality weak. Some day it arranges its limited number of words into a new thought, a bad thought, our idle mind grasps the significance of the new thought, and we give birth to a new piece of scandal, or we commit a crime. The brain is pleased, because the execution of the new bad impulse brought more blood, more vitality to it, and it gets the habit of thinking bad thoughts and conveying evil impulses. They were the product of idleness of mind. And as a matter of statistical fact, all tragedies, crimes, vices, scandal, gossip and misery are direct products of mental inertness or idleness.

The minds of the grumbler, the gossip, the thief, the criminal, are poor, empty, starved, wayward minds, and their brains are small, poorly nourished, sickly brains. The young wife with a moment of leisure who has a starved, empty mind, is a victim of her passions, her[Pg 377] surroundings and her ungoverned impulses. The young wife whose brain is being fed by the study habit, is self-contained, is master of her impulses and her passions. The mental latitude of one is limited to caprice, envy, discontent, hate and jealousy; the other is light-hearted, charitable, just, contented, and happy.

Shut the two in a dungeon and the owner of the starved, empty brain will go mad. The other will find hope in her heart, and in her brain, the children of her thoughts will troop in, bringing solace and cheer and courage.

From a practical standpoint the study habit has an economic value. It preserves health and peace of mind, it enhances efficiency, it broadens our sympathies and charities, and it unifies the home circle. It is an easy habit to acquire, and it sustains its interest: it is inexpensive. The Carnegie libraries, correspondence schools, the university extension plan of lectures, etc., contribute in a large measure to its easy acquirement, and to the success with which it may be pursued.

Two Ways of Gaining Knowledge.—We gain knowledge in two ways. First, by experience, which means mingling with people, exchanging ideas, discussing topics, listening to lectures, sermons, talks, etc. Second, by reading and studying. We must read and study in order to really understand and assimilate what we learn from experience, and what we hear discussed in lectures, sermons and talks. As soon as we become interested in a study we begin to rise above what we may call the everyday plane. We desire to know more, and when we know a good deal about one subject, we want to know something about kindred subjects, so we extend the latitude of our knowledge. It is marvelous how the habit grows. It is not work, it is pleasure. We long for spare moments to renew the study, and as we experience the pleasure the growth of our mind affords, we improve in all directions. Every cell in the brain sends out vibrant impulses, new life, new hope. Health means more, life has a meaning. We find happiness in the company of those who are striving for higher ideals. We perform even our menial tasks with more care and[Pg 378] with more interest, because we grasp their true meaning, and we know that we cannot aspire to higher ideals if we are dishonest in little things. So the study habit makes better men and better women of us, and it adds to the pleasure of life all the real pleasure there is in living. The power to analyze, to conceive, and to create are the highest pleasures mankind possesses, and they can only be attained in any degree by education and cultivation.

It is not easy to explain to the average superficially educated person the satisfaction to be derived from original or creative thinking. One must progress far enough in mental self-culture before it becomes a pleasure, almost an intoxication. Up to a certain point the acquirement of knowledge is a task, an effort, a seeming self-sacrifice; beyond that point it is a labor of love, a pleasure, a consecration. The crude, discordant efforts of a child, when it first begins to acquire a musical education, very convincingly illustrates the condition of mind of the beginner in self-culture. The task is a toil and the results do not stimulate further spontaneous effort. The same child, however, may successfully pass through the various gradations of a musical career and arrive at a time when effort will submerge itself; when the result of the knowledge acquired will be so gratifying that it will no longer be a toil; when the study will be pursued because of the actual pleasure it affords.

The only worthwhile thing in life is mind. If one does not develop the mind, it is possible to live an entire lifetime and not really live at all. To exist is not to live. All the amenities of life contribute to existence, not to life itself. To live is to create, to give, to endow.

If a book contains one original thought, it will live. Few books contain more than one thought, one inspiration. If it, however, suffuses that one thought into the hearts of men its existence will have been justified. We have no criterion or standard by which to judge the ethical value of a thought. If a thought conveys an inspiration to another and is productive of moral growth it has life and value because it creates.

To exist is to blindly follow the primal instincts. To[Pg 379] live is to think, to reason, to grow mentally. Consequently we must have ideals, we must cling tenaciously to these ideals, and, "We must know what we want."

The Young Wife's Incentive to Self-Culture.—A young wife has a real incentive to self-culture if she hopes to maintain her position in the home and in the affection of her husband. A man has always the advantage of being actively engaged in one of the two ways of acquiring knowledge. He mingles with people. He gains considerable knowledge and frequently cultivation unwittingly. He grows with his business, and as it increases he becomes more important in the community. He mingles with keener, wide-awake business men, his wits are sharpened, his brain must be alert and virile. A healthy active brain grows, it is responsive, it absorbs knowledge. As he climbs higher, he wears off the crude corners and assumes a worldly cultivation, which men of sound business sense can adapt to suit any social exigency. The wife does not have these advantages, and, unless she appreciates this point, she is very apt to remain where she was when she married, so far as mental culture is concerned. Now to be wife in a true sense, she must be companion. She must keep pace with his prosperity on the one hand and with his intelligence on the other. The more culture and knowledge a man attains the more critical he becomes, the more cultivated his tastes, the more cultivation he demands. Qualities that did not always grate upon his sensibilities become acutely objectionable in his higher mental state. A man may be loyal at heart, but he resents the inaptitude of a wife who fails to keep the mental pace. He is willing to give his wife the benefits of his material prosperity, but he cannot give her the finer evidences of his higher mentality, because, while she may have proved true as a wife, she failed as a companion. She fell behind in culture. He cannot give that which she cannot receive. The young wife should appreciate the difference between moral disloyalty on the part of her husband, and mental disloyalty. He is the transgressor in the first, and she is the culprit in the second delinquency. We must meet a situation as it exists. Moralizing[Pg 380] does not change the conditions. A man and woman may be temperamentally suited to each other to-day, and in a few years may be wholly dissimilar in tastes. If being a wife simply implied more loyalty and domestic efficiency there could be no just cause for complaint if she failed in every other respect, but it does not. To be a wife more than in name, one must be friend, companion, confidant. No one, much less a husband, selects as a friend, companion, and confidant, an individual whose tastes are not in sympathy with his own, who does not understand the viewpoint, one in whom he cannot confide, or one whose intelligence is crude. A man can obtain a housekeeper anywhere, but he cannot buy a home-maker, a companion, a friend, or a confidant.

The study habit will create the interest. If you once get it, only death can take it from you. If you become interested, no man can grow away from you, and no man can take from you the worlds it will open up. You must, however, begin the study habit with the determination to acquire knowledge. You must want intensely to succeed, and you must be willing to sacrifice self, and to work diligently. "If you quit, it simply shows you did not want an education, you only thought you did,—you are not willing to pay the price."

Nosophobia, or the Dread of Disease.—There is one disease I would warn the young wife not to acquire. It is called nosophobia. It is without doubt the most serious sickness with which any member of the human family may be afflicted.

In another part of this book I have written the story of the aged philosopher, who, on being asked to name the worst troubles he had in life, answered, "I am quite sure my greatest worries, and my worst troubles were those that never happened." This reply is well worth thinking about; it contains matter for serious reflection, and what makes it so suggestive and valuable is that it can be proved true by the experience of our own lives.

Nosophobia means dread of disease. It may astonish many to know that such a condition is regarded as a disease, and that it has been given a name. Instead, however,[Pg 381] of it being a rare disease, or an unusual condition, we find it is one of the commonest diseases, and one of the most easily acquired conditions. In fact, it is so easily acquired nowadays that we have to be constantly on guard against it. Though we may not be its victim, we have all felt its influence at some time, and even one experience of it is sufficient to satisfy the most exacting. It is an absolute medical fact, that the dread of disease will render one more profoundly miserable and unhappy, and will cause more mental and physical incompetents than will any severe, prolonged, actual sickness. People who are victims of nosophobia are probably the most miserable and wretched individuals on earth. This is essentially so because of the peculiar characteristics of the disease. It is an insinuating and insidious ailment and its progress is cumulative. When we begin to worry about our health the germ of nosophobia takes up its habitation in our midst and we never know another happy moment.

The dread of disease is probably more common now than it used to be, partly because people know more about it, and, therefore, have more material out of which to manufacture dreads, and partly because a large number of people have the leisure to worry about various symptoms and sensations that come to them, and the significance of which they exaggerate by dwelling on them until they become positive torments. It is particularly those who have not much to do, and, above all, those who have absolutely nothing to do who suffer most from the affection. Children never suffer from this malady because pains and aches have no significance to them. The probability of death through sickness never bothers them. Their minds are always occupied. They are always busy, they think only of life and of living. As we grow older, however, we become introspective and we permit conditions to favor the development of a wrong mental attitude. We accentuate the seriousness of each trifling pain and illness, and the specter of death looms up in the path of each ailment. Soon we spend needless time in worry and we imagine we are not as healthy as we ought to be and that we may probably die in the near future. This affects our temperament and our efficiency. Life is no[Pg 382] longer tolerable or attractive, and we shortly are numbered with the failures and the incompetents.

One of the unfortunate consequences of nosophobia is that a victim of it not only renders her own life miserable, but she unfortunately affects the happiness of every member of the household. She is as a rule gloomy and morose, and this constant depressive environment is not conducive to the success of any effort toward creating moments of amusement and happiness. Her presence acts as a deterrent and repeated failures to overcome this domestic cloud finally result in a complete cessation of all effort. Things fall into a rut and each member of the family seek their various forms of diversion outside the home circle.

These individuals are sometimes spoken of as "trouble seekers." In a sense, the term is appropriate, because the troubles which wreck their peace of mind never occur. In the beginning there is usually some slight physical ailment. As a rule, it is some form of nervous indigestion. Under appropriate and adequate treatment such forms of indigestion are readily curable in ordinary individuals, but these patients are not ordinary individuals. They are perverse and opinionated. They have their own ideas. It is impossible to convince them that they are not as sick as they imagine. They think the physician fails to quite comprehend their cases,—that he does not recognize the serious side of the ailment, and so they are never wholly satisfied with medical assistance. The little incidental pains of the indigestion are indications of heart disease to such a patient and she acts in sympathy with this awful affliction; the real explanation being that the gas produced by the indigestion bothers the heart for the time being. She is very apt to diet as a consequence, one article after another being avoided until she is living on a starvation diet. She fails to appreciate the fact that she needs more nourishment, not less; that her stomach is in good condition, the fault being with her nerves. She finally becomes anemic and neurasthenic and a misanthrope.

The young wife can readily appreciate that, to expect domestic success and happiness under such circumstances, would be impossible. Yet there are young wives who develop[Pg 383] this habit of accentuating their little pains and ailments inordinately, to their husbands, on every occasion. They adopt this dangerous means of exciting extra sympathy and caressing. Some do it in explanation of their failure to perform their household duties efficiently—a laziness plea pure and simple.

These inefficient and tricky little ladies find that it is easy to impose upon their unsuspecting husbands, so they proceed to work out the details to their own satisfaction. After spending the day sight-seeing or shopping or gossiping, and having neglected their work and feeling tired, they assume a becomingly abandoned position on the big, new, comfortable couch, practice a few heartbreaking sighs and experiment with the tear supply. These details are arranged and timed to be effective just as Jack opens the hall door with the latchkey. We can picture what follows without making any effort to dramatize the incident. But if the reader will try to create mental pictures of the frequently recurring home-comings under the same circumstances, she will develop interesting studies in domestic psychology as she watches the effect upon Jack when the truth begins to dawn upon him.

It needs no oracle to assure these women that they are traveling along a road that has only one ending. Love is as old as the hills, and the older it gets, like the wise old hills, a wiser old love it becomes. It exacts its price, and its price is an equal love. There never was a love born—except maternal love—that will sustain itself after the knowledge dawns upon it that it is being bartered away and imposed upon. The day of reckoning comes in time and the dream is over.

Do not forget that the first year of married life is the trial year—the real test of your soul-merit. During that first year you carve, as it were, on a monument, in a thousand different ways, the ineffaceable record of whether you deserve success and happiness in the struggle of life. In what should be the after-glow of love's young dream—the first precious weeks and months as a young wife—no element will be more subtly dangerous than the art of duplicity. Before a young wife determines to practice deception she should fully appreciate[Pg 384] the inevitable consequences. If, under the mistaken idea that she can easily deceive her husband, because "he trusts me so," she believes she may continue to do so with impunity, she is the most elementary of all silly little fools. She has failed to observe that the great law of the universe acts in the interest of the rich and poor, the fool and the philosopher alike. She will become too clever and like all fools and criminals she will give herself away. She will wake up to find that she has been playing with the sacred things of earth—home and a husband's love; that, never again can she reëstablish the affection and confidence which she has trampled upon and defiled; that the future is a mortgaged hope and she herself an unclean and unworthy thing.

Practicing the art of duplicity in simulating physical ailments will, if persisted in, establish nosophobia. The patient will come to believe that she is not exactly well. She will establish the habit of feeling sick. This will render her mind diseased and the diseased mind will in turn suggest new and additional aches and pains, and she will soon not know whether she is sick or well. The dread of disease will effect its retribution and soon she will be, in fact, an unhappy and an unsuccessful young wife.

Modern conditions unfortunately favor the easy development of nosophobia in young wives. Our larger knowledge of the symptoms of diseased conditions tends to render the analysis of localized pain more definitely and more suggestively. Certain pains, we are told by hearsay busybodies, mean certain serious conditions, and the category of these diseases extends from indigestion to consumption and to cancer. To the victim of nosophobia this suggestive knowledge is a constant terror and an ever present nightmare. To the normal healthy mind they mean nothing and suggest less.

The modern young housewife has a superabundance of spare time. The utilization of the young wife's spare time is of the most momentous importance as we have previously pointed out. It is the one commodity which will speak in the after years in words of solace and cheer or in regret and condemnation—according to how these[Pg 385] precious moments are spent. If these moments are not spent in a way best fitted to wholly occupy the mind, the mental attitude—to which we previously referred, and which is conducive to the cultivation of nosophobia—will have been developed.

There are certain kindred conditions that may partly explain, to the ordinary healthy person, the real distress of mind into which these self-centered sufferers sink. The fear of a thunder storm, for example, creates profound dread and distress of mind in some people. The dread of dirt, of sharp instruments, of certain insects and animals, of darkness, of an ocean voyage, and of great heights, are common examples of this type of mind-distress of which the characteristic symptom is an inexplicable and uncontrollable dread. The same system of self-discipline and self-control is necessary to effect a cure of these various forms of mind-distress as is necessary in the successful treatment of dread of disease. To none of these other forms, however, is attached the same degree of seriousness by the laity as they attach unjustly to nosophobia. The conditions are all the same, but they reason that the dread of darkness or dirt or mice or height cannot possibly bring death or seriously affect the health or happiness, while sickness and the dread of it, means—so they imagine— pain and maybe death. Medically, nosophobia has no such significance. The condition exists only in the mind and the same effort at self-discipline will cure the dread of disease as well as the dread of any other possible condition. It is this element of mind, however, that lends itself to the cure of this condition by other means than legitimate medical advice and so we have had "healers" and "miracle workers" who have sprung up from time to time in the history of the world, who have cleverly taken advantage of this element in human nature, and reaped a rich reward.

"Keep Still and be Well."—To instruct the young wife how she may guard against acquiring this habit, we would suggest that she "keep still and be well."

When the world appreciates better the psychology of thought, its tremendous significance will have a concrete meaning. We are too apt to regard the thought we[Pg 386] give utterance to as a meaningless thing, so far as its influence is concerned. The woman who harps upon her ailments, who appears at the breakfast table with a depressed and melancholy visage, who regales us with an account of how poorly she slept, the nightmares she experienced, the pain she suffers, and who puts into her inflection the poison of self-pity is an emissary of Satan. I have seen a whole family's happiness for the day destroyed by the meaningless ranting of a hysterical woman. Life is hard enough for all, for each of us to at least wish each other well.

The individual who cultivates the habit of carrying sunshine and good cheer to the breakfast table belongs to the sort of folk who help and inspire the whole world to a greater achievement. If one is sent away each morning from home with a cheery word and a radiant good-by he is inspired with the virtue of success and his efficiency is ensured.

Cultivate the art of contentment and remember that relationship does not imply liberty; you have no right to send out into the world a member of your family depressed and miserable because of your irritability and evil habits.

"Keep still and be well." If you cannot say a good word about a fellow-being, say none at all. Don't become a scandal-monger. We can forgive those who talk evil about us—they talk to hear themselves talk. The gossip germ is born of ignorance and vacuity and breeds best in idle minds. No one is influenced by the vaporings of a gossip, her words die in empty air. She injures herself only. The loquacious pest who brings to us the tales which the scandal-monger manufactures is the one who robs us of our peace and is unforgivable. To dignify the malicious intentions and idle nothings of an evil mind by carrying them further is an expression of degeneracy that is urgently in need of active disinfection. To vilify another is foolish; to repeat it, is the function of a rogue. Your friends bring you the glad tidings of the good things that are said about you: your enemies are those who, in the holy name of friendship, bring to you the poison of evil gossip. "Keep still and be well."

[Pg 387]

THE HOME

[Pg 389]

CHAPTER XXVII

"If we are eager to do something to lighten the load of another, eager to sacrifice self; to cheer, and counsel, and inspire; to leave unsaid some unkind word, to forget our own troubles in the larger trouble of a friend, we are home-builders."

"A married woman can't decently spend her life in playing bridge, and in running ribbons through her underclothing She hasn't any right just to camp on her husband's trail.

"No woman on earth has a right to maintenance unless she gives value received."

DOMESTIC QUALITIES

A Good Housekeeper and Home-maker—What Constitutes a good Housekeeper—Preparation and Selection of Meals—Washing Dishes—Pots and Pans—Dusting and Cleaning—Work Cheerfully and Be Thorough—Don't Be a Dust Chaser—Don't Get the Anti-sunshine Habit—Air Your Rooms—The Ideal Home—The Medical Essentials of a Good Meal—What Makes the Home—Working for Something—The Average Housewife's Existence Is Slavery—What Shall We Work For—Making Ends

Meet—Rest and Recreation—Try a Nap—Get Enough Sleep at Night—Go Out of Doors—Take a Vacation Now and Then—Life Insurance—Owning a Home—The Cheerful Wife and Mother—The Indifferent Wife and Mother—Husband and Wife.

A Good Housekeeper and Home-maker.—If the young wife carries out the suggestions made on the preceding pages and thereby contributes her part to establishing the material success of the co-partnership, will she profit in any other way?

She will have become a good housekeeper and home-maker.

Housekeeping is an acquired art, home-making is a moral quality, an instinct. Housekeeping conducted as an art is superfluous. Home-making is a triumph under any circumstances. There are many good housekeepers; there are few competent home-makers. Housekeeping may easily be overdone; home-making can never be overdone. A beautiful house is not necessarily a[Pg 390] beautiful home. Housekeeping should be conducted with a view to home-making and never for any other reason. Sometimes we see housekeeping brought to its highest perfection by the same woman who never did understand the simplest rudiments of home-making. The woman who becomes the victim of the housekeeping mania never realizes it; it is an insidious art.

There can be no doubt that a well-kept house is a thing of beauty. So also is a marble statue, but it is cold and bloodless.

The young wife must strive to combine the two faculties. She should be an efficient housekeeper in a happy, comfortable home.

What Constitutes an Efficient Housekeeper?—An efficient housekeeper is one who has acquired the knowledge necessary to perform all the duties of housekeeping, and who executes these duties efficiently, with the least possible expenditure of time and labor.

It is an absolute fact that most young wives begin housekeeping with the crudest ideas as to what housekeeping means. It has been pointed out many times, that many mothers bring their daughters up without instructing them in the elementary principles of keeping house. It is nevertheless necessary to repeat this statement over and over again, and to point out the enormity of the injustice done. Even if a daughter is fortunate enough to marry a man who is capable of supplying all the help necessary, a wife should know enough to intelligently discern if the work is properly done. If she does not understand the rudiments of housekeeping, and has no help, her inefficiency may be directly responsible for breaking up the home.

Preparation and Selection of Meals.—Thoroughness and simplicity are the two essentials to a satisfactory meal. If the articles are thoroughly cooked and the selection simple, there is no chance for trouble. A breakfast of fruit, a thoroughly cooked cereal with cream, a boiled egg and toasted bread and butter, is simple and is adequate. Freshly prepared hot biscuits sound good, but, unless you know your oven and have had a lot of experience, they are apt to result disastrously. Even[Pg 391] if you are an expert, don't make them. They are very bad for digestion.

For dinner, lots of thoroughly cooked vegetables, a small piece of steak or two lamb chops, bread (at least one day old), and good butter, a baked apple, stewed prunes, or rice, boiled for three hours, is enough for any one. Have your meals on time. Be sure the table cloth and napkins are clean, and your dishes hot. Establish the habit of being cheerful at meals, of eating slowly, and of coming to the table with a clean, fresh dress.

Washing Dishes.—While your husband is reading the evening paper, wash your dishes. Washing dishes is an art. Few young wives acquire it. The secret is, a big basin, lots of hot water, lots of soap, and a desire to wash them clean. If you wash them clean, don't smear them over by drying them with a greasy dishcloth. Wash your dishrag and drying towel every day, and hang them up to dry in the sun.

Pots and Pans.—How they are neglected! If you have any pride as a housekeeper, be clean. Hot water, soap, a cleansing powder and a little effort, and your pots and pans will be a credit to you. Have a system. Take time. Keep your kitchen tidy. Don't let work accumulate from meal to meal or from day to day. It is astonishing how lazy and dirty some women are. We have seen young women on the street, dressed tidily and smartly, and we have gone into the homes of these women and have been disgusted and nauseated with their general appearance. There is absolutely no excuse for this, and a young wife who gets into the habit of being indifferent is a disgrace to her sex. She cannot hope for success or happiness.

Dusting and Cleaning.—Every home should be thoroughly cleaned once a week. A certain day should be selected for the purpose. A certain system should be followed. After it has been done a number of times, you will devise ways and means of doing it quicker, easier and better. New methods will suggest themselves from time to time, so, by planning and systematizing, you will get rid of the drudgery part, and there will be a constant incentive present to beat your past record. You[Pg 392] must get rid of the feeling that it is uninteresting drudgery and slavery. A woman who looks upon her work in that light is not deserving of any better fate, and she will not get much further. If you are one of these perverse individuals who resent advice; if you object to being told the truth; if you do not want to profit by experience; if you are satisfied as you are, don't waste your precious time reading books. No author can tell you how to get something for nothing; no teacher can instruct others in anything. He can only awaken thought and arouse impulses. The law of life is harmony. An individual who wastes God's precious time in grumbling and fretting is the most pitiful object in the universe. Try to appreciate that you are part of the divine problem, regarding the conduct of which certain implacable laws have been formulated. To obey these laws means continued life, health, strength, power and success; to disobey them means weakness, sickness, incapacity, unhappiness, discontent and premature death.

Some people learn quickly how to conserve strength, how to systematize, how to be cheerful and hopeful and to radiate thankfulness. From a selfish standpoint this is the only method that pays. Some people will not see the point. They will put it aside by some such sophistry as: "Oh! it does not apply to me." It does, nevertheless, and probably at a later date, when the chance of achievement has withered, they will see the point through the mist of regret.

Work cheerfully, therefore, and be thorough. Don't overdo it. Fussiness is objectionable, useless and unhealthy, because it is a constant drain on nerve energy. Some women are dust-chasers.

They are eternally poking into corners with a feather duster. They chase dust from one room to another and back again, and the sight of a few grains on the piano makes them sick. Dust with a moist cloth and when your dusting is over leave it and forget it. Don't buy a feather duster.

Don't get the anti-sunshine fad. Let the sun in. Don't pull your shades down to save the parlor carpet. Your husband would probably sooner buy another than pay for a funeral.[Pg 393]

Air your rooms always, night as well as day. You cannot overdo it. Buy mosquito screens, keep the flies out, but let the air in.

The Ideal Home.—It is difficult to describe an ideal home, but we know one the moment we are in it. Its atmosphere instinctively breathes the personality of the home-maker. Its individuality distinctly differentiates it from the ordinary impersonal home. Its housekeeping dress is inviting; its furnishings harmonious; and it exhales repose, and comfort, and peace. When we meet its mistress we are welcomed in a low, gentle, cordial tone of voice, and in a manner which radiates honesty and unaffected simplicity. We discover the source of the unusual atmosphere. It is herself, the wife, the mother, the home-maker. She is the mystery of the ideal home. Each day her divine art grows more perfect because her heart is consecrated to the work. She may not be surrounded with material splendor. The miracle is in the soul she possesses. Love is the magic wand she yields. She loves her home, her children, her husband. She is the queen mother in the paradise she creates.

We have seen that a good housekeeper may not be a home-maker. Every home-maker, on the other hand, is a good housekeeper. The ideal home could not exist unless presided over by a home-maker. A home-maker necessarily implies being a good mother; but a good housekeeper, who is not a good mother, will never be a home-maker.

A good housekeeper will keep house for the art's sake and will resent any domestic event which upsets her housekeeping sense of decorum, even though the event may have splendid home-making possibilities. The mother with the home-making instincts will invite, and aid, and will conceive events, which, though they upset her housekeeping routine, will contribute to the happiness and edification of the home circle. The housekeeper's sense of duty ends when a good dinner is served; the home-maker's real duty and incidentally her pleasure begins, when dinner is on the table.

The Medical Essentials of a Good Meal Are: Pure food, judiciously selected for two reasons. First, that[Pg 394] there may be an adequate daily variety—in order to stimulate the individual taste and appetite; second, that the food supplies may be adapted, in nourishing equivalents, to the work and age of the diner. The food must be thoroughly cooked, eaten slowly, and masticated with care and deliberation. Every meal should be served and eaten when cooked and ready. Food should never be allowed to stand when cooked to the proper degree. Overdone food is not desirable. The dishes should be heated to the proper degree; the table linen, napkins, etc., clean and fresh; and the family should all eat at the same time.

A meal should never be hurried. Interesting conversation is, therefore, a necessary and a commendable feature while dining. There is less desire or tendency to hasten through a meal when one is interested or is being entertained. The intervals between courses will be welcomed rather than resented under these circumstances, and the appetite will be keener and the enjoyment greater.

The wife and mother, who is the home-maker and consequently responsible for the *esprit de corps* of the family, will direct, suggest, and guide the conversation into profitable and interesting channels. By thus supplying the atmosphere necessary to the efficient eating of a meal, the digestion and the assimilation of the food will adequately take care of itself. Overeating is never a part of any meal and should be religiously avoided.

What Makes the Home.—We know it isn't the house we live in that makes the home. Many have lived in humble dwellings and have carried all through life the memory of home as a sacred legacy. Wealth does not make a home, nor culture, nor any of the intellectual attainments for which we may strive unceasingly. We may have all these and yet not know the joy of "home." "Home" conveys to every heart the same tender memories. To have known the blessings of a "home" is to be fortified for life's battles. No one can deny its importance in humanizing mankind. A boy who has never known what it was to have a home, whose substitute for the home associations was an "institutional mother," may[Pg 395] have all the necessary potential qualities for success, but he will be forever deprived of the inspiration that memory of home kindles in every human soul.

The secret of the sources of home is its atmosphere. The atmosphere of home is the sum total of the kinship and sympathy radiated by its members. It is a tangible something which is capable of being felt, which is capable of inspiration and which is capable of being carried away into the years beyond, exerting a helpful influence over the milestones of worry, and trouble, and defeat; and it is always a fragrant, soothing, energizing influence. Every human heart needs the memory of a home and the presence of a friend at all times and in all places.

We must contribute our share to form the right kind of home-making "atmosphere." The two qualities which are essential to this task are sympathy and peace. Each contributor must be more than a negative unit in the home. It is not enough to simply desire peace—a deaf mute could fill that part. We must desire to please and we must be an active agency working for harmony and peace. If there is in our heart enough sincere affection for brother and sister, father and mother, the desire to please will be the bond of sympathy that will weather every temperamental storm. If we are eager to do something to lighten the load of another, eager to sacrifice self, to cheer and counsel and inspire, to leave unsaid some unkind word, to forget our own troubles in the larger trouble of a friend, we are home-builders. We must control our moods in the home, we must submerge the instinct of selfishness, of impatience, of pride, and of obstinacy. We must not be opinionated, we can many times conform to the opinion of others in trivial matters and preserve peace; we thereby minister to the happiness of others, because to give happiness is the surest way to be happy. Temper is the sting that poisons many homes. Its possessor is an impossible associate and will defeat the work of the angels in the effort to make homes.

Working for Something.—At various times we have emphasized the necessity of having definite plans, of "knowing exactly what you want," of "beginning wedded life with ideals";

in other words, we believe that to combine[Pg 396] the maximum efficiency with the greatest degree of happiness it is necessary for all of us to "work for something."

It is not necessary to prove that the average human life is uninteresting; most of us know that. As a matter of fact the average existence is a monotonous, hopeless dreary stretch of time, dotted at more or less frequent intervals with physical pain and suffering, and with mental sorrow and anguish.

While this is undeniably a true epitome of the average life to-day, it is not to be accepted as the only possible average existence. Every agency that is working for the betterment of the conditions which surround life is helping to elevate the status of the average individual. As individuals, the question whether our life will conform to the average, or be individualized, rests with ourselves.

The ordinary average housewife's existence is slavery in its loneliest and most wretched form. Its utter hopelessness is its most depressing feature. If we could hope for some glint of sunshine, some day in the future when conditions would change, some circumstance which would give us the opportunity which we have never had, some test of our womanhood,—anything to relieve the crushing, hopeless inertia of the daily routine,—we imagine we could go on again, hoping that things would permanently change eventually. Don't "hope things will change." Change them! Don't get in a mental rut; don't be an "average" housewife. If you really can't do anything else, if things are so abjectly hopeless that there is no other way out, if your path is leading to nowhere, start a rebellion. When the smoke has cleared away you may see a new path to follow, and it may lead to somewhere. It is not necessary to do this often, because the fault is usually our own, and not that of environment or conditions, or our husbands. All we need to do is to think things over, and begin something, and all the other conditions will take care of themselves. The moment we step outside the humdrum path of existence, the moment we are curious enough to do this, there is hope for us. A little mental fresh air will dissipate a good many brain fogs. The instant we begin "working[Pg 397] for something" definite, we cease to follow in the procession of the average helpless and hopeless citizen. So to the young housewife we would strongly suggest that she "think things over" and decide what she is going to work for.

Now, what will it be? Of course it will be different with each housewife. With many it will be "a home of our own." It may only be a piano for the children, or it may wisely be more insurance. Possibly you live in the country, and you long for the social and other advantages of the city. You may be a city wife and may long for a farm in the glorious country. It may be a trip to Europe; or a college education for the boy; or a musical career for the daughter. It does not matter what it is, the "it" is the thing itself, and, having found it, the world for you has changed. The lonesomeness, and the hopelessness, and the wretchedness of life have disappeared. There is always in the future the "it"; no matter how dark and gloomy the road may be, it is illuminated at the far end with the realized "it." It is the bearing of the burden of life that makes a wife, and when we have "something to work for" we begin to live. Love is the explanation. We don't want the home for ourselves. We want it for those we love, we want those we love in the atmosphere, which I, as mother, will make in "our home." It is the elemental mother that speaks,—the motherhood spirit that pours out eternally in self-sacrifice and keeps no debit account. It is the cry of the primal mother that echoes through all the ages and which has kept the race sane and safe and hopeful. Having something to work for supplies the element necessary to cheerfulness. In the darkest moments, when everything seems to go wrong, the thought that we can look forward to a time when a great change is coming, when we will move to the new home, when we go to the farm or the city as the case may be, or when John will finish his college course and start out as a lawyer,— when the strain of skimping and making ends meet is over we feel that the struggle will let up and we can rest in peace for a little while. It is sharing these burdens that counts, and brings out the best elements of human nature. The struggle[Pg 398] of making ends meet draws the young couple closer together, and adds that touch of divinity that is essential to confidence and love. It strengthens character, curbs the tendency to unnecessary expenditure of money and time, and teaches frugality and patience. The incentive to win out is ever present, and it is the anchor that means final satisfaction and success.

Try to see the point. Work for something,—something worth while, and when you have once begun never turn back. "Nothing-succeeds like success."

Rest and Recreation—A young couple should find time for rest and recreation as well as for work. This part of the domestic problem should be carefully and systematically utilized, and just as faithfully carried out as any other part. Both husband and wife should participate in these hours of enjoyment, and the husband should assiduously try to make of these respites periods of real mutual benefit. No matter in what station of life one may be, it is always possible to find congenial means of passing many happy and profitable hours together, if the spirit of companionship and mutual interest is kept alive. It is the incessant strain upon the nervous system that constitutes the real danger of home life. The struggle to make ends meet; to keep the children neat and well fed; to look respectable; to provide clothing and education; to nurse the sick; to tolerate gossipy neighbors; to put up with ugly tempers; to meet the constant drain of society, business, politics and religion,—the wonder is that so few remain outside the lunatic asylums.

There are certain inevitable daily happenings in the life of every housewife that must be tolerated though they are not pleasant. A certain number of interruptions will come at the most inopportune moments. The children will come in with muddy feet and walk over the clean floor; some days the stove works splendidly, other days it acts as if it was crazy; the milkman is late to-day and too early to-morrow; some days the iceman comes, some days he stays away, and these are the days we want him most; the upstairs work is not quite done when cooking must be begun; the grocer forgot to send the butter; a dish or two will crack or break every day; doors will[Pg 399] slam; the rain begins to fall just when the clothes are all hung out; baby needs nursing just when the pie must be turned; a visitor calls before the dishes are washed. These are inevitable. The cure does not lie in some impossible revolution. We must rest the nerves and take the strain off.

Try a nap in the middle of the day. Lie down and relax even if you do not sleep. In some countries this is a national custom. It should be a law in America. One cannot appreciate the amount of good that can be gained from one-half hour's sleep. Medically it is a wonderful rejuvenator.

Get enough sleep at night. Late hours in the home is a bad habit and a poor investment. It affects the health and the efficiency. One extra hour means all the difference between frayed-out nerves, exasperated dispositions and home peace and contentment. There is a certain fixed ratio between sleep and good nature that has been formulated into a law by psychology. Keep early hours and the whole complexion of life will improve.

When indoor work becomes irksome go out of doors, try a walk. Nothing will dissipate tired-out nerves quicker than a brisk walk. Every housewife should walk in the open air every day of her life. It is an absolute necessity if she hopes to retain her health and spirits. She will be in better shape and in a better mood to carry out her part of the daily programme.

Take a vacation now and then. Go to the seashore or into the mountains. When a housewife is run down and irritable; when the disposition comes to indulge in a lonely cry; when she wishes she had never been born; when the cook stove and the children are hysterical irritants; it is time for a day off. The husband should find time to take his wife into the country for a week end, even a day at the seashore will work like magic.

Resting and recreation are necessary. If we do not recognize this fact, and adopt the habit as a preventative, we will be compelled to take it in an effort to cure a malady that has established itself as a consequence of the neglect. It, therefore, is a time and money saver, and it saves friction, and home, and maybe life.[Pg 400]

Life Insurance.—Every young wife should insist upon her husband carrying life insurance upon his own life. She should make this a part of the prenuptial agreement. We would go further and state that a man who will not willingly agree to this is not a safe man to marry. The kind of insurance is immaterial, so long as it guarantees to the wife an adequate sum of money in the event of his premature death. The wife should regard the payment of the premiums as one of the necessities, and should personally know that they are promptly paid.

Owning a Home.—It should be the hope of every married couple to own their own home. It has been the regret of many, when in later years they have figured up the money which they have spent in rent, that they did not think of this plan earlier. Nowadays, it is possible to pay a very small sum down, and certain monthly payments, which apply on the purchase of a house. By beginning this way, when the family expenses are small, it is comparatively easy, and without any deprivations, to own the home outright in a few years. Many couples foolishly buy gaudy and unnecessary furniture, and live in more expensive homes than their means justify, in order to create an impression, when first married, which they later regret. If part of the money, which the young husband has undoubtedly saved,—or he should not marry,—was paid down on the purchase of a house it would be paid for before the extra expense which necessarily comes with children had to be met. The plan works to the advantage of the couple both ways, because, if no rent has to be paid out after a few years, the extra expense of children would not then be a hardship.

The Cheerful Wife and Mother.—How many happy memory pictures we see by simply reading the name,—the cheerful wife and mother,—we might call her the optimistic mother. No matter what we did as children, we were never afraid of her. She always saw the bright side, and if we did something wrong she never scolded angrily; she talked to us convincingly and made us slightly ashamed of ourselves. If we had any plan or project we took it to her, she listened, and she suggested, and before we knew it she had solved our problem and the plan[Pg 401] was possible,—away we would go, enthusiastic and happy, to work out the details as she suggested, and shortly our "party was on its way." If any of us had an accident,—we didn't go home, we were afraid of a scolding,—the victim was rushed to her, she would wash the blood and tears away, bathe the wounded part, put on a bandage and then take the little patient up to her room. A cake and a story would soon have us feeling good and help us forget our pain. Oh! she was an angel to us. On rainy days she found a way to amuse us, our dirty feet didn't count, the floor was to be washed up anyhow. To keep in her good graces, however, we had to be reasonably good. She told us stories, and we soon found out that she didn't like a mean or stingy boy, and a boy or girl who would tell a lie she would not talk to for a week. Her stories always proved that the mean boy, or the bad little girl, or anyone who told lies, never had a good time, that no one liked them, and most everybody kept away from them, if they didn't stop being bad. She was a wonderful mother, and every boy and girl for miles around knew her and loved her.

And so it is that children soon learn who their real friends are. A home is what the mother makes it. Cheerfulness does not cost anything, and how much better it is if happiness abounds. You can get infinitely more of the confidence of a child by being gentle, and by showing that you have his or her real interest at heart. They will trust you more and rely upon your forbearance in the event of anything going wrong. As we boys and girls grew up the interest of the angel mother didn't cease; we met her often, and she would ask "how things were going." She knew exactly what each of the boys and girls was doing, and we always told her the truth, and all the truth. If anything did go wrong, she would know of it from one of the others, and she would "look up" the unfortunate one. Many times to my knowledge she has helped another mother over a crisis; when a boy was about to go wrong or showed a tendency to do some foolish thing. She did so because she "had a way" of getting round the boy, that even his own mother did not possess, and he would listen. A mother who can preserve[Pg 402] her own cheerfulness under all circumstances is a jewel. The influence she wields is beyond estimation. A radiant cheerfulness is something akin to Christlikeness, it is an inspiration. People who live together frequently feel out of sorts in the presence of each other without a feeling of compunction, without realizing that they are guilty of a social discourtesy. If there is in that home an optimistic, cheerful mother, how different the atmosphere is! The cross look, or the touchy word, is quickly observed and all the power of her infectious cheerfulness is brought into battle array and the discontent is chased away, the vitriolic spirit of quarrel, slumbering so near the surface, is made to feel ashamed of itself. It shrinks into the darkness, and we begin the day all over again, thankful that mother is so good, so considerate and patient.

It isn't exactly by the children that such a mother is best appreciated. Father knows the real value of her cheerfulness. He knows just what it has meant in the past, and he knows what it means now. He can look back and he can recall many instances in which the optimism of his wife was the agency which turned the tide. He knows of many business deals wherein the cheerful advice of his wife changed his viewpoint and so changed failure into success. He can recall many instances during the early days of his business career when the outlook was gloomy and doubtful, when its success depended upon so small a matter as temperament and disposition, when the cheerfulness, the love and tact of his wife dispelled the gathering clouds, strengthened the wavering spirit and instilled new fight, new purpose, new hope, into the situation. Oh, yes, he knows that cheerfulness, and optimism, and tact, and love, have a definite economic value, but it cannot be estimated in dollars and cents. He knows they are an asset in the domestic problem, but they are sacred, holy, consecrated.

Cheerfulness is such a potent reality that it has a definite, concrete value. Life is a product of environment to a very considerable extent. Our surroundings very often dictate our attitude, and temperamentally at least we radiate whatever spirit our environment generates.

HEREDITARY FEEBLE-MINDEDNESS[B]

Here is the law. The blood of the father was tainted. For several generations it lay dormant, and then smote this little child, Bertha. It is the terrible, the inevitable law of heredity.

Not so much now, as years ago, is there intermarriage. It is fortunate, for the results of in-breeding are far worse in human beings than in animals; chiefly because of man's more highly developed nervous system. New, pure blood above all things else is a re-energizing force which may go far toward eventually eliminating any trace of taint.

[B] "Feeble-mindedness; Its Causes and Consequences," Goddard, The Macmillan Company.

[Pg 403]

One cheerful home will radiate, will send out into the world, certain definite, concrete influences which will encourage and stimulate, and strengthen and give new hope to every living thing it reaches. The atmosphere of cheerfulness will exert a specific influence upon every disposition within its zone. The children of a cheerful mother and home will radiate happiness, contentment and love. The husband of a cheerful wife will carry into life's struggle a more just, a more equitable, a more humanizing influence as a direct, concrete result of that cheerfulness, and who can tell into how many other homes the spirit of cheerfulness will be carried as a consequence of the justice, and equity, and charity of that husband and father? To return after a day's work and worry to a fireside, to a home, in which cheerfulness is the radiating element is to inspire contentment and peace and thankfulness. Out of the joy of thankfulness, out of the satisfaction of peace, and the fulness of contentment, the kingdom of Heaven is born, and when human hearts feel like this they are living near the borderland of great possibilities. The cheerful wife and mother needs little advice. She does, however, need our love and the knowledge that we are true to ourselves and that we are fighting an honest fight. She will be happy in that knowledge.

The Indifferent Wife and Mother.—The home over which an indifferent wife and mother presides is a "happy-go-lucky" home. There is something radically wrong in the make-up of a woman who is wife and mother and who is indifferent. It is not a natural condition, and it is frequently a product of simple ignorance. Such a woman may be exceedingly amiable and charitable; she may take an active interest in church and social affairs, and may be regarded as a kind and model housewife. Her interests are outside the home, however, and since the home is a place of apathy and indifference she feels she must "keep busy" elsewhere. She is out of touch with her husband and his affairs, and the children "get along somehow." If they come in for meals and report for bed that is all "any one can expect." There is seldom any acute friction, because every one is[Pg 404] indifferent and selfishly attends to his own affairs.

Such a home is devoid of the domestic atmosphere. The mother touch is lacking: sentiment and love have long ago taken wings: the temperature of the place is cold and forbidding. The children "exist" and may be healthy animals, but their souls are empty and there is no comradeship or affection in their make-up. They do not know what human sympathy means, and they either grow into successful machines, or indifferent citizens. As human beings they are failures. It would be astonishing to know how many of this type of mother and wife the present strenuous age is producing. They are certainly on the increase, and the unrest, which is a growing characteristic of the sex, is tending to still further increase this type of womanhood. The mother element is being subverted and in its place we find "Justice" with her scales, but with a marble heart.

These women do not realize that the citadel of motherhood is a sacred, holy citadel, and that its responsibilities cannot be met by a negative allegiance. A child's character, its training, its physical equipment, its mental development, its body and soul, its heredity and acquired instincts, its virtues and its vices, its environment, are all mothers' cares, mothers' duties, mothers' responsibilities, and if they are neglected part of the eternal scheme is frustrated and recompense will be exacted. When a woman marries she assumes responsibilities which she cannot and dare not neglect. If she does, she will have to give an accounting of her stewardship.

The indifferent mother and wife does not fit. She is incompetent, she is one of nature's sarcasms. She is a mistake as a wife, as a mother, and as a member of society. She is not sincere or she would not be guilty of such fundamental injustice. As a human being she is a parasite, and in the Master's vineyard she is a weed.

Husband and Home.—As sponsor for the welfare and efficiency of the family and the home, the wife and mother should occasionally give some thought to the husband and father.

William Muldoon, one of the greatest physical efficiency experts in this or any other country, who has intimately[Pg 405] known hundreds of our great men in every walk of life, recently stated that American men to-day do not appear to have the same amount of physical endurance and nervous energy that men of forty years ago possessed. In other words, as a race we are degenerating. In his opinion the condition is due to the fact that commercialism has taken such a firm hold upon the American people that everything else is cast aside to make a success in business or profession.

This is a serious indictment coming from such a source and should be of intense interest to the wife and mother of to-day.

The over-worked business man, when he gets into the hands of the physician, is a neurasthenic. He has gone just as far as his vitality will take him. His mind is fagged and worn out and will not concentrate. He is nervous, irritable, and wretched. His appetite is capricious, and he sleeps fitfully. For a few days he pulls himself together and plunges into work, but the effort exhausts him and he falls back further than before. He is unhappy and despondent, his viewpoint changes and the future looks uninviting and he loses his courage and his faith in himself. He hides all this from his family, he does not want wife and children to know that he is losing his hold. He even makes desperate efforts to keep fit while at home, and for a time he succeeds.

All this has been brought about by tremendous concentration of effort to do ten times as much work as he should do, and it has all been done in order to acquire riches and independence, not so much for his own sake as for his family's sake.

Now, a wife who fails to see the handwriting on the wall is no wife at all. Any wife who cannot tell, by a single look, exactly how her husband feels is not quite what she should be. Some women may question this declaration. They may regard it as a far-fetched indictment. The truth nevertheless is,—and all good citizens are thankful that it is so,—that if a man and woman live together for years, and during that time work together in sympathy and love, and share the burdens of life together, they grow toward each other; there is a psychic[Pg 406] force that binds them so that when the clouds begin to settle over one the other promptly sees the mist and brings all her subtle skill and solicitude to guard and fight in the other's interest. The "two hearts that beat as one" are old hearts, hearts chastened by experience and mellowed by the sorrows and joys of life, hearts that have gone through the dark spots and the deep spots of affliction, and have loved and helped each other all through the long journey to sunset's old age. God never inspired a holier picture than the wrinkled face of a good old mother. The old eyes, with the peering promise of a near peace in them; the toothless mouth, whose words of cheer are records of the past;

the wrinkled face, the sad token of human frailty; the gentle word of welcome which age trustingly bestows, all speak to younger hearts with hungry words, and we hope that their lot is one of peace and contentment and happiness.

A wife, therefore, who has shared the burdens of life honestly and willingly with her husband will promptly note when life's struggle is becoming dangerous to her helpmate.

The true wife will insist on rest, and quiet, and recuperation. No man has the right to sacrifice himself for his family and no family should dare to expect it. A wife should frequently inquire and find out what their success is costing her husband, find out the price he is paying. No success is worth while if a man is undermining his health and strength to attain it. Men do it, however. American business men do it all the time.

Maternal sacrifice is admittedly the supreme or Christ-like instinct of the human race, and it has been accorded the glory which is its due, but the unsung song of father love is a more pathetic incident of this strenuous age than we are apt to believe. America is building a breed of men with a dual passion, the passion for riches, and the passion to protect. The one is a wrong ideal, the other is a wrong principle. Ask any of the worn-out men who are inmates for the time being of the splendid institutions in the country devoted to the recuperation of health: ask the medical superintendents of the large sanitariums; ask Muldoon; ask the busy men of big business[Pg 407] why they keep in the harness after they have made enough to retire upon; why they strive and fight and sacrifice themselves, and you will be told that the force which impels them is the desire to protect, with ample fortune, wife and children, and those dependent upon them. The average well-balanced man of America is never happier than when he can give to his loved ones every comfort and luxury possible. He is willing to work and so sacrifice self to the utmost to consummate his ambition. The right kind of a wife will see that her husband is getting a square deal.

The right kind of solicitude and the right kind of argument will tend to divert her husband's attention away from business, to the advantage of all concerned. The children of America need closer fellowship with the fathers. We should read fewer tales of the profligacy of rich men's sons and less lurid accounts of the doings of the daughters of society. The sons of poor men would profit by a freer companionship with the more experienced father, and the daughters would be less apt to wander away from the fireside of a home that was knit together by the broader sympathy of father love.

The training and education of our children is far more important than storing up money for them to spend recklessly. We all need help and cheering words and encouragement to do justice to ourselves and others. Nothing will inspire and stimulate youth more to achieve, to be clean in mind and body, and to succeed, than the knowledge that he is loved, and trusted, and has the implicit confidence of parents and of brothers and sisters. His pride is awakened, he would hate to fail, or to disappoint them, so he makes a conscientious effort to be worthy and to succeed.

The mothers are at the helm. They must be the harmonizing factor in the home, and they must bring their human ships into safe harbors. The storms and the battles of life will only unite the crew together if the "captain" is the right "man" in the right place.

[Pg 409]

CHAPTER XXVIII

"All that I know, I owe to my mother."

Abraham Lincoln.

HOW WE CATCH DISEASE

We Catch Disease—How Germs Enter the Lungs—How Germs Work in the Body—The Function of the White Blood Cell—How an Abscess Is Formed—The Evil Habit of Spitting in Public Places—Sunlight and Germs—Why It Is Necessary to Open Windows—Facts About Tuberculosis—The Tendency to Disease—The Best Treatment for Tuberculosis—Consumption Is a Preventable and a Curable Disease—When Delay Is Dangerous—What to Eat and Wear in Hot Weather—Scientific Dressing—Drink Plenty of Water—What to Drink When Traveling.

A simple explanation of how we "catch" disease may be interesting and profitable. Let us take, for example, a case of consumption. In order to "catch" consumption it is necessary to breathe into our lungs the germ of consumption.

How do we "catch" these germs?

If a consumptive patient spits or expectorates on the street, or on the floor of a railroad car, or in a room, or store, or theater, after a time the spittle becomes dry, and because of the wind or a breeze which may be caused by opening or shutting a door, or it may be the skirts of women walking about, the dried sputum in which the germs are becomes mixed with the dust of the air. If we happen to be around, just at the particular time when the germs are blown into the air, we may breathe into our lungs enough of them to produce consumption. If we are in good health, and if we do not happen to get too large a dose of the bacteria at one time (and that is only a matter of luck), we can overcome them, as will be shown shortly. If, however, we are not in good health, if we are just recovering from some serious or depressing disease, such as Grippe, the bacteria will overcome our reserve vitality, and consumption will graft itself on our weakened system.[Pg 410]

How do these germs work?

They lodge on some part of the lung tissue and burrow into it. They make a nest for themselves and begin work immediately. They live on the lung tissue, they multiply rapidly, they produce—as a result of their activity—a poisonous substance. Because of their eating up, as it were, the lung tissue we often find holes (cavities) in the lungs of consumptives. By breeding rapidly they require more and more room, so they invade more and more of the lung tissue and destroy it. The poisonous substance which they produce is absorbed by the blood. Its effect on the blood is to weaken it, and when the blood becomes weak the vitality declines, so that the patient loses weight, appetite, and strength. The poison also produces fever, and so the long, weary fight goes on till death claims the patient.

What Happens If We Inhale These Bacteria, and Consumption Does Not Develop.—In order to understand the answer to this question it is necessary to explain certain facts concerning the white blood cells. The white blood cells can pass through a blood vessel and back into it again without leaving any hole in the wall of the blood vessel.

The function of the white blood cells is to wander around and if they discover any stray bacteria, whose presence is undesirable, it is their duty to get rid of it as quickly as possible. The white blood cell may therefore be likened to a detective whose duty it is to arrest any suspicious character who comes into the city. When a white blood cell discovers a strange microbe it immediately surrounds and encloses it within itself, just as your hand can enclose any small object, such as a cent or a dime. It then promptly goes to the nearest blood vessel, enters it, and is carried away in the blood stream. If we are in good health our blood cells are alert, active, and capable of defending us against any invading foe in the form of a microbe or bacteria. If we are not in good health the bacteria may overcome the white blood cells. If we inhale a large number of the consumptive bacteria at one time, and they succeed in getting into the lung substance, they are immediately met by an army of blood[Pg 411] cells, all bent on capturing them. An actual battle is fought and the deciding factor of the battle will be the condition of the patient. If there is plenty of strength and reserve force, if the patient is in good health, the blood cells will win the battle; if the condition of the patient is poor, the blood cells will lose the battle and tuberculosis, or consumption, has its beginning in that patient from the time the blood cells lose their fight. We know the battle has been lost because the well-known symptoms of the disease soon appear. The blood cells do not retreat when defeated; they go on fighting to the best of their ability. Whether they ever succeed in overcoming the bacteria, depends upon the treatment the patient gets, and his personal conduct. We give him a maximum of fresh air and sunlight because these are the great enemies of all kinds of bacteria. We force his feeding and try to stimulate his appetite, hoping thereby to give him strength so that his blood cells will fight actively in his interest. We take steps to reduce his fever so that his strength may not be wasted and burned up. If we succeed, with the necessary active coöperation of the patient, the blood cells finally overcome the bacteria and the patient recovers from the disease.

This is the story of the invasion of almost every disease. It is the story of the white blood cell.

The white blood cell is active in another way and it is a very interesting way. When you cut yourself the blood cells immediately surround the entire cut. They line up like an army defending a city. They form a perfect wall, millions of them, ready to pounce upon all enemies in the form of bacteria or microbes, that have the temerity to try to creep into the wound unseen.

This is the reason that so very few of the hundreds of little surface wounds and scratches which every one gets, ever become infected or go wrong in any way.

When a microbe does get inside, under the skin, and becomes active, as they sometimes will, the white blood cell, appreciating that it cannot defeat the enemy, begins to build a wall around him and locks him in. This compels the enemy to limit his activity within the wall, which he does, and so an abscess is formed, which bursts[Pg 412] when the bacteria fill it so full that the wall gives way and empties the poison out on the surface of the skin, thus saving the body from the poison of the microbe which would spread all through the body, were it not for the wall formed by the active, busy little white blood cell.

The foregoing simple explanation of "how we catch disease" will no doubt be suggestive to the interested and careful reader. The first and most obvious question that suggests itself is: If we "catch" tuberculosis by inhaling germs from some other person's dried spittle, why are consumptives allowed to spit where it will do harm? Consumptives are not allowed to spit where it will do harm, but they do and they always will.

Every department of health in every civilized corner of the globe has secured the enactment of laws making spitting unlawful in any public place. Every sanitary society, every agency whose aim is to work in the interest of public health, has actively aided, and is aiding, in the propaganda for a better universal understanding of the principles of sanitation and hygiene. The individual must be educated to understand the tragic need of such a law. You cannot legislate virtue into the public conscience. It is a profound reflection upon human intelligence to appreciate that the great white plague, for the stamping out of which so many thousands of lives are annually sacrificed, and so much money is spent, could be forever stamped out, if the human race would agree absolutely to stop spitting.

It is the duty of every person to take an active personal interest in this crusade of education and emancipation. We appreciate and concede that a large number of those afflicted with consumption do not willfully spit, knowing that others may be affected as a consequence. They do it in ignorance. Our aim is to educate the victim to an understanding of the true condition. The knowledge must be carried into every home, and the story must be told in a simple, convincing way, to attain results. The mothers of the country can aid to a very considerable degree, in this commendable work. Every mother can tell her children the story of how disease is caught. She can tell them that the danger[Pg 413] spots of infection are where people congregate together, in church, school, theater, street-cars, and railroad trains. She can teach them to breathe through their nostrils, especially when in these public places, because the nostrils are so constructed that they act as a sieve or strainer, they clean the air we breathe, and when we blow the nose after being in one of these places we blow out thousands of germs and other impurities which would have gone straight into the lungs if we had breathed through the mouth. She can teach them the value of deep breathing when in the open air, and of standing and walking erect so as to get all the lung space possible. By constantly reminding children of these little points you will be amazed at the progressive improvement which goes on both in their bodies and in their minds. They will become little missionaries, they will tell the story to others, and a real good can be accomplished in this simple way, that will grow in strength and vigor as the years roll round.

The next suggestive feature in the reading of "How we catch disease," is the significant emphasis which is put upon sunlight and fresh air in the treatment of consumption. Sunlight, as already stated, is the great enemy of microbes and germs of all kinds. Where sunlight is, germs do not want to be. How wrong, therefore, is the habit of lowering the shades, when the sun shines into your home, because it "spoils the carpet." Let it spoil the carpet; it is much cheaper to buy a new carpet than to pay for a funeral. Let the sunlight stream into your rooms for the few hours it can every day. Germs love the dark, sunless corners where the dust is. Housewives should, therefore, go into the dark corners with a moist duster, and wipe them clean, then boil the duster and hang it in the sunlight to dry until needed again. If you choose to use a feather duster instead, as the lazy woman does, you only chase the dust and the germs from one corner to another, and in doing so you afford yourself the opportunity of swallowing a few germs in the passing. One may, therefore, be punished in an unexpected way for being lazy.

For the very excellent reason that corners and angles[Pg 414] are unsanitary, there are to be no more of them in the construction of houses and office buildings of the better class. They are being built with "round" corners; even the ceiling and walls, and floor and walls, meet in a curve,—no square crevice or corner where dust or germs can gather.

If we add moisture to a sunless spot, we have the ideal environment for germs to breed and flourish in. There is always moisture or humidity in the air if the altitude is low, and if it is near the ocean, or any large body of water, the moisture is relatively greater. For this reason we send patients with pulmonary disease to the mountains, where the altitude is much higher, where there is no moisture, and consequently where there are practically no germs. We cannot move our homes to the mountains, however, so what must we do to get rid of the moisture and the germs where we are compelled to live? What do we do with the family wash when it is wet? We hang it up in the yard, in the sun and in the breeze, because we know from experience that the wind and the sun soon dry anything wet. They do more; they freshen everything, so that anything exposed to the sun and air smells fresh and sweet and is fresh and sweet and pure. So to make our homes sweet and fresh and dry we must chase the stale air away, and the moisture with it, by opening our windows and letting in the sunlight and the breeze, every day, and for as long as possible every day. Open windows and sunlight and fresh air,—all you can get,—this is the song of health, the joy of life, the only agents that will keep the eager, busy, little white blood cell healthy and willing and alert. This is the reason you must keep the windows of your bedrooms open at night, as well as by day, so you and your children will get fresh, pure, sweet air, and not stale, moist, germ-laden air to breathe.

FACTS ABOUT TUBERCULOSIS

Tuberculosis, or consumption, is a disease of poor air, dusty quarters, insufficient nourishment, and, above all, of ignorance with regard to its dangers and what we now know of the possibilities of its cure. The more we know[Pg 415] about it the better chance there is to cure it, and better still, prevent it.

Not very long ago the death rate from consumption was one in six, that is, every sixth person who died in this country died as a result of tuberculosis in some form. It is now about one in eight. This is a remarkable decrease—about one-third of its former ratio of victims are now spared. Not so very long ago the disease was regarded as practically fatal; now it is classified as one of the eminently curable diseases. The universal dissemination of this knowledge will do much to rob the "Great White Plague" of its terrors.

Investigation and observation have demonstrated that there is in the great majority of people a definite tendency successfully to throw off the disease. It is a curious and astonishing fact, which we have learned from the study of the results of autopsies; we find, in nearly every instance, that every person in whom death occurred after thirty had had consumption at one time and resisted it and died of some other disease. We mean by this that at some time, in all likelihood during one of the "colds" of childhood, every one of us contracted consumption, but because of our vitality we successfully resisted and conquered it. In other words, the white blood cells won their fight.

This knowledge is of great value; it taught the scientists who were studying the characteristics of the disease that there were conditions, possible of attainment, under which the human organism could definitely and victoriously defeat the invasion of the tubercle bacilli.

The public mind, until recently, was imbued with the fallacy that the disease was hereditary. It was thought that if it "ran in the family" the victims of it were almost certain to die. We know definitely now that consumption is not hereditary, and that, instead of death being certain in a patient in whose family it has been, this fact alone ensures the victim a much better prospect of cure than if it had never existed in the family. The explanation of this seeming paradox is quite logical from a medical standpoint. The theory of the vaccine treatment of disease is that if you infuse into the blood the[Pg 416] products of the germs of certain diseases, the individual in whose blood the vaccine has been put, will wholly resist that particular disease, or if he acquires it, it will be in a mild and more modified form. If a family for a number of generations has had various members die of tuberculosis, the blood stream of the family will have become so impregnated with the toxins, or poisons, of the disease, that, in time, a certain immunity will have been established. Consequently, tuberculosis in an individual, the blood of whose ancestors has been accustomed or habituated to the poison of the disease, will run a milder course, be more modified in its type, and will respond to treatment easier than in an individual whose family history is free from the taint of tuberculosis.

In proof of this principle, it is a well-known fact that consumption runs a rapid, fatal course among those nations which have not hitherto been exposed to it. The death rate among our American Indians when it was first introduced among them was enormous.

The same truth applies to syphilis. The blood of the civilized race has become so thoroughly syphilized, that it is no longer so susceptible to the disease as it once was: and the disease as we know it to-day does not manifest the same virulency as it did years ago, or as it does in a race in whom it is grafted for the first time.

These ideas of the curability of the disease and of its non-heredity are extremely important and supremely suggestive. Tuberculosis takes only the quitters and the supine. Anyone who will fight bravely against the disease can always resist its ravages for many years, if not to the extent of living out a normal life.

The Tendency to Disease.—Mothers should understand just what is meant by "the tendency to disease." We assert that consumption is not hereditary, but we know that certain individuals are born with the tendency to tuberculosis. Just what does this mean?

Let us suppose a tubercular mother gives birth to a child. It would be foolish to assume that this child comes into the world with a normal standard of resistance; but it is certain he is not tubercular and doomed[Pg 417] at the moment of his birth. He may be what is ordinarily termed a weak, puny, sickly infant, but the germ of disease is not implanted in his constitution. If he is taken from his mother, taken away from the tubercular environment, and brought up under the best hygienic and sanitary surroundings, it is possible for him to become a robust, healthy, normal man.

The tendency to disease in this case will not materialize. If, however, we permit him to remain with his tubercular mother, to nurse her milk, to live in what necessarily is an unhygienic and unsalutary environment—the presence of the consumptive mother renders it so—the probability is that the tendency to disease, which in his case is the tendency to weak lungs, will materialize, because of his weak resistance, poor nourishment, and unfavorable surroundings. If, therefore, his method of living does not contribute to building up and strengthening what is in the first place a weak structure, the structure itself will, during the first strain put upon it, give way, and naturally the weak spot will be the point of election for the invasion of disease. This strain may be one of the infantile diseases,—scarlet fever, or measles, or whooping cough, or it may be bronchitis. Instead of convalescing from these conditions, as a normally constituted child will, this child, whose potential resistance is below standard, will fail to reach the rallying point, will afford a fertile field for germ invasion, and will develop tuberculosis,—not directly, however, as a result of having had a tubercular mother, but because he was not removed from the tubercular environment and given a fair chance. The high infant mortality is, to a very large extent, caused directly by this "tendency to disease," plus unfavorable environment, and this is wherein the eugenic propaganda has found its field of promise and is unassailable reason for active existence.

Let us take another illustration, so that mother may have a full understanding of the far-reaching effect of the "tendency to disease."

We cannot justly assume a child to have outlived its hereditary tendencies until it has reached the period of its full growth, physically, mentally, and morally. We[Pg 418] know that this period is about the twenty-third year. Now a young girl of eighteen, or even twenty, who is successfully resisting an inherited tendency, is likely to reach her full physical and mental growth, providing she does not subject her vitality to a serious physical strain, or providing she is not the victim of a serious illness. Suppose this young girl marries and becomes pregnant; this condition immediately changes the fighting or resisting equation; she is no longer conserving her strength and energy; she is spending it out, wasting it so far as it applies to her own upbuilding. The percentage in favor of a successful fight against the inherited tendencies is greatly reduced, and as a matter of fact, statistics show—as is fully explained in the article on "The Evils of Early Marriage"—that many of these young mothers succumb to disease as a result of pregnancies at this period of immaturity, when they could have otherwise lived. The "tendency to disease" has therefore an economic value and the state should build along the line of the conservation of health in its broadest sense.

The Best Treatment for Tuberculosis.—The most important factor in the present-day treatment of consumption is the right kind of nourishment. This cannot be emphasized too strongly. In the first edition of this work, it was stated that the most important factor in the treatment of this disease was fresh air. The author has had very good reasons to change his opinion radically in this respect.

So emphatically may this truth be asserted that it is now not at all necessary to seek a change of climate in the hope that such a change may aid the patient. It must not, however, be understood that this reasoning applies to charitable cases. If the patient is so situated that it is not possible to provide a proper environment, a change may do good. It is not the change of air that is responsible for the improvement, however, though it no doubt contributes in these cases; it is the altered environment.

Patients who in their own homes enjoy sanitary and hygienic care; who may have a room of ample size for their exclusive use, which is thoroughly aired, day and night; who are provided with the "right kind of nourishment,"[Pg 419] and who will obey implicitly the rules which the physician, who is conversant with this particular method of treatment, will lay down, may be assured that a prompt response will ensue. The intelligent reader will understand that this statement does not apply to patients in the last stages of the disease. The assertion, however, must rightly be regarded as revolutionary. It is not what we were taught—it emphasizes, nevertheless, what every physician already knows, that, theoretically, consumption is a disease that should respond to treatment. That we have not had greater success with it in the past, must be attributed to our method of treatment. The fact that most of us have had the disease, and have recovered, conclusively demonstrates its curability. Those individuals who fail to recover promptly do not possess the vitality to throw it off spontaneously. If at this time—the real beginning of the disease—it is discovered, and the right treatment instituted, we immediately supply the organism with the ingredients it is deficient in and we are justified in looking for favorable results if the patient adheres to the instructions.

The second essential in the treatment of consumption is an abundance of fresh, pure air. We therefore direct the patient to remain in the open as much as is possible. If circumstances permit him to sleep out-of-doors, so much the better; if not, he must sleep in a room with the windows open to the fullest extent, winter and summer. There are no exceptions to this rule. If it storms, the outside blinds may be closed, but the windows must remain open. The city air is just as efficient for our purpose as is the air of any other vicinity—the point is, to get enough of it from a mechanical standpoint. The advantages from sending patients away, even under the old belief, were more than discounted by conditions incident to the new environment that were detrimental to their progress. Now that we know it is not necessary or essential to procure any other kind or quality of air than exists in any city, all our efforts may be concentrated in the interest of the patient in directing the "right kind of nourishment" and in supervising his conduct. In few instances is it necessary to prescribe any medicine.[Pg 420]

In exceptional cases the cough may require some sedative remedy, especially if it disturbs the patient at night. Experience has taught us, however, that to live twelve hours in the open air and to sleep with the windows wide open, will do more for the cough than any medicine we possess.

Pleuritic complications may cause pain, but this feature is best aided and permanently relieved by fresh air also. Very recently there were made exhaustive experiments in this connection in St. Thomas' Hospital, London, England. It was decided to subject patients to open-air tests for pleuritic pains in the course of consumption. This particular hospital is situated on the River Thames, in a notoriously damp and foggy part of the city; despite this drawback it was conclusively shown that the patients who lived night and day on the balconies breathing this heavy, murky, damp atmosphere, were relieved of their pains quicker, and more permanently, than those who were shielded in the wards of the hospital.

Inasmuch as the patient must be adequately nourished, his cure depends upon the condition of the stomach. It is known that the germ works more actively in a patient who is losing weight. When the germ is very active, its poisons, circulating in the blood, cause fever and fever results in tissue waste. We must therefore bend every effort toward overcoming this tendency. If we can get the patient to take sufficient food and if he digests it thoroughly, the weight will increase, the fever will subside, and the tissue waste will stop. Patients must be extremely careful, therefore, what they put into their stomachs. Only simple, tasty, highly nutritious food should be taken, and digestive energy should not be wasted on less nutritious materials. For this reason incalculable harm has been done by indiscriminate medicine-taking. Medicines exert a bad influence on the stomach and those patients who take them lose their appetites. Drugs should never be taken except for a definite purpose and only on the advice of a physician. These patients should particularly be guarded against the use of advertised patent medicines. They are always bad, and never under any circumstances are they of any advantage,[Pg 421] as is clearly shown in the chapter on "Patent Medicines." Thousands of persons die of consumption every year who would have lived had they not taken such remedies.

The following article is sent out by the New York Department of Health as a Circular of Instruction regarding Tuberculosis.

INFORMATION FOR CONSUMPTIVES AND THOSE LIVING WITH THEM

Consumption Is Chiefly Caused by the Filthy Habit of Spitting.—Consumption is a disease of the lungs, which is taken from others, and is not simply caused by colds, although a cold may make it easier to take the disease. It is caused by very minute germs, which usually enter the body with the air breathed. The matter which consumptives cough or spit up contains these germs in great numbers—frequently millions are discharged in a single day. This matter, spit upon the floor, wall or elsewhere, dries and is apt to become powdered and float in the air as dust. The dust contains the germs, and thus they enter the body with the air breathed. This dust is especially likely to be dangerous within doors. The breath of a consumptive, except when he is coughing or sneezing, does not contain the germs and will not produce the disease. A well person catches the disease from a consumptive only by in some way taking in the matter coughed up by the consumptive.

Consumption can often be cured if its nature be recognized early and if proper means be taken for its treatment. In a majority of cases it is not a fatal disease.

It is not dangerous to live with a consumptive, if the matter coughed up by him be promptly destroyed. This matter should not be spit upon the floor, carpet, stove, wall, or sidewalk, but always, if possible, in a cup kept for that purpose. The cup should contain water so that the matter will not dry, or better, carbolic acid in five per cent. watery solution (six teaspoonfuls in a pint of water). This solution kills the germs. The cup should be emptied into the water closet at least twice a day, and carefully washed with boiling water.

Great care should be taken by consumptives to prevent their hands, face, and clothing from becoming soiled with the matter coughed up. If they do become thus soiled, they should be at once washed with soap and hot water. Men with consumption should wear no beards at all, or only closely cut mustaches. When consumptives are away from home, the matter coughed up should be received in a pocket flask made for this purpose. If cloths must be used, they should be immediately burned on returning home. If handkerchiefs[Pg 422] be used (worthless cloths, which can be at once burned, are far better), they should be boiled at least half an hour in water by themselves before being washed. When coughing or sneezing small particles of spittle containing germs are expelled, so that consumptives should always hold a handkerchief or cloth before the mouth during these acts; otherwise the use of cloths and handkerchiefs to receive the matter coughed up should be avoided as much as possible, because it readily dries on these and becomes separated and scattered into the air. Hence, when possible, the matter should be received into cups or flasks. Paper cups are better than ordinary cups, as the former with their contents may be burned after being used. A pocket flask of glass, metal, or pasteboard is also a most convenient receptacle to spit in when away from home. Cheap and convenient forms of flasks and cups may be purchased at many drug stores. Patients too weak to use a cup should use moist rags, which should at once be burned. If cloths are used they should not be carried loose in the pocket, but in a waterproof receptacle (tobacco pouch), which should be frequently boiled. A consumptive should never swallow his expectoration.

A consumptive should have his own bed, and, if possible, his own room. The room should always have an abundance of fresh air—the window should be open day and night. The patient's soiled wash-cloths and bed linen should be handled as little as possible when dry, but should be placed in water until ready for washing.

Rooms should be cleaned daily, but in order to prevent the raising of dust, all floors must be well sprinkled before sweeping, and all dusting, etc., done with damp cloths.

If the matter coughed up be rendered harmless, a consumptive may frequently not only do his usual work without giving the disease to others, but may also thus improve his own condition and increase his chances of getting well.

Rooms which have been occupied by consumptives should be thoroughly cleaned, scrubbed, and whitewashed, painted, or papered before they are again occupied. Carpets, rugs, bedding, etc., from rooms which have been occupied by consumptives, should be disinfected. Such articles, if the Department of Health be notified, will be sent for, disinfected, and returned to the owner free of charge, or, if he so desires, they will be destroyed.

When consumptives move they should notify the department of health. Consumptives are warned against the many widely advertised cures, specifics, and special methods of treating consumption. No cure can be expected from any kind of medicine or method except the regularly accepted treatment, which depends upon pure air, an out-of-door life, and nourishing food.

Consumptives having an opportunity of entering a sanatorium, should do so at once.

[Pg 423]

When Delay Is Dangerous.—Inasmuch as it is mother's duty to watch over the health and the efficiency of all members of the household, she would do well to establish a rule to err on the safe side in every case of sickness. That rule should be never to delay too long in obtaining medical aid.

In nearly twenty years of active general practice I have had hundreds of "hurry" calls to "come at once." In not over a dozen of these calls did any of the cases demand immediate attention from a medical standpoint. Most of them, however, should have had earlier aid. People wait too long in the hope of spontaneous recovery, and when, instead of recovery, they realize that the patient is quite sick, they become conscience-stricken and send a "rush" call for the doctor. After delaying from day to day they decide to get professional advice and send a messenger for a physician with instructions to "go for another if he can't come at once." It is imperative he should come instantly, though they have delayed for a week in requesting his services. Every physician has these calls every week of his life. If an individual has survived a week's neglect, it is quite within reason to assume that he will survive another hour,—and during that hour the physician may have time to complete whatever he may be doing when the call comes.

If you have been guilty of bad judgment in not sending earlier for aid, don't add discourtesy to your sins. The world demands of us, and every person has the right to expect, a certain degree of consideration and courtesy. If we do not give it, we only harm ourselves because the lack of cultivation is a detriment which limits growth and happiness. The degree of attainable happiness is limited by the degree of "goodness" that is in us. If you are not considerate, depend upon it, there is an element of happiness which escapes you, and you cannot attain it till you are considerate.

It is inconsiderate and it is discourteous to send an immediate demand for a physician "to come at once" if there is no urgent need for his services, and if you have just been inspired for aid after a week's blindness, there[Pg 424] is no urgency in the matter. A call in an hour would do just as well.

Take the following case: A mother discovers a small quantity of blood in the diaper of her two months old baby. There is a larger quantity in the afternoon and she decides to give the baby a dose of castor oil. During the night it slept fitfully and in the morning it has a large stool as a result of the castor oil and there is a large quantity of blood in the stool. She sends a "rush" call for a physician. The physician discovers the following facts: The baby is being artificially fed; it has been vomiting its food for a week; its stools have been green, foul and contained mucus; it had a fever for a number of days; it has lost much weight and looked pale and sickly. The physician obtained this history from the mother—she therefore knew the baby's condition. Why did she delay sending for a physician? How sick did she want the child to be before the need for aid seemed justifiable to her? Why didn't the sight of blood in the stool suggest the need of assistance? What do the public expect of physicians in such cases? But why ask questions? Many mothers will doubt the existence of such a mother as is described above. They need not; she was one of my own patients. I do not understand such women; I only know that such mothers exist in quite large numbers. This particular mother has other children; she is a good housekeeper, is personally attractive, and is thought well of in the community. If such seemingly heartless conduct can spring from such a source is it not evidence of the fact that the average mother needs instruction, needs education, and does it not bespeak the need of eugenics being sown broadcast throughout the land?

Delays are dangerous in all sicknesses that last, despite a thorough cleaning out of the bowels. To wait, hoping that "things will change," is bad practice. It is unjust to the medical profession, and it is infinitely more unjust to the victim.

There are two kinds of surgical operations—those of choice and those of necessity.

Every one knows about the operations of necessity,[Pg 425] most of which must be performed as a result of accident, but few people understand the dangers of delaying what are termed "operations of choice." These are for such conditions as appendicitis, cancer, and stomach and bowel troubles.

Delaying an operation of choice lessens the chances of living, and really makes an operation of necessity with fewer chances of recovery than from the operations that must promptly follow injuries.

When we feel that an operation is needed, or are in doubt about it, the wise thing to do is to consult medical authority. Then, if it is found there should be an operation, there is plenty of time to make every arrangement. We can begin to diet, which is generally necessary and there is every chance for speedy recovery.

If a man breaks a leg and it has been set badly, the surgeons do not rebreak it at once, but allow it to heal and the patient to regain his strength, when it is again broken and reset properly. This is an operation of choice.

But if a terrible fracture of the leg results from a fall, with the shattered bone protruding, an operation of necessity must follow to mend torn arteries.

It has been learned through recently gathered statistics that about thirty per cent. of the people operated on for appendicitis die simply because they delay the operation. This should have been an operation of choice, when every arrangement could have been made long beforehand; the delay makes it an operation of necessity, with the victim in such poor physical condition that he has not half the strength to recover that he would have had if he had been wise enough to consult a physician when he first suspected that something was wrong.

These same statistics go to show that fully 99 per cent. of the appendicitis cases, when taken in time, are cured by means of the operation, thus affording the strongest proof of the folly of delaying such things.

The total number of deaths from appendicitis each year, due to delay in operating, is greater than the number of deaths during the Spanish-American War. There are instances where the doctors do not advise operations soon enough.[Pg 426]

Above all things, when a reputable physician advises operation, do not think you know more than the physician, but have the operation performed at once. Nine times out of ten this will be the means of saving your life.

WHAT TO EAT AND WEAR IN HOT WEATHER

No faith should be placed in the so-called "hot-weather" foods. The cereals and other manufactured foods advertised as possessing marvelous qualities, have in reality no advantage. Some of them have more or less value as ordinary food, but they certainly possess no unusual superiority. Home cooking is the best in summer or any other time.

Great care should be taken to keep the system in the best possible condition. This will prove the most effectual safeguard against the heat. Some foods do not agree with certain individuals, and these should be carefully avoided in summer. Every person will have to judge for himself in this matter. Otherwise the diet should be balanced carefully so that enough, and yet not too much, is eaten. As much fruit as possible should be eaten, and meat never more than once a day. It is not well, however, to omit it entirely.

Food sustains the body through the heat it generates chemically, and it is therefore impossible to eliminate a certain heating effect. If the system is kept normal, however, and the diet properly balanced, this should not be felt. Work is performed by the body and energy expended. This must be replaced with the heat value of food. A certain amount of fat, starch, and the other constituents of a well-balanced diet is essential.

Fat meats and other forms of fat are the most heating of all foods and may be minimized in summer. The amount of food necessary is, of course, largely governed by the nature of the work performed by the individual. Brain workers can eat very little in the morning and during the day, reserving until evening the single heavy meal. If they have been doing this the year around they probably will be cooler during the morning and afternoon[Pg 427] if a light breakfast and luncheon are eaten. It is not well, however, to make any radical change from one's regular habits.

Manual workers require more food, and the heavy meal had best be eaten in the middle of the day. All three meals should be substantial. There is no danger of eating too much if the system is not overburdened.

Not only is pork rich and fat, and therefore very heating, but it is the quickest of all meats to spoil. Veal also spoils very quickly if not kept at the proper temperature. Of all meats mutton has the best keeping qualities. Beef also keeps well and is a safe meat to eat in summer.

Flies are dangerous under any conditions, but particularly should they be avoided where meat is kept. The bacteria they carry thrive particularly on meat, and therefore are apt more rapidly to multiply than if deposited on some other food. Care should be taken to buy meat only from places where adequate protection is provided against flies.

It is of the greatest importance to keep the meat at a uniform cold temperature. It should not be allowed to become heated, and then cooled again. Some meat shops still keep the meat on open counters or hooks and replace it in the refrigerators at the close of the day. These shops should be carefully avoided. Modern methods provide glass-covered refrigerating counters which keep the meat cool while it is on display.

Meat should be kept at as low a temperature as possible. The ordinary refrigerator is at a little above freezing and temperatures at or below zero are preferable.

Scientific Dressing.—By dressing scientifically it is possible to minimize the effect of the heat. The heat from the sun must be kept away from the body and the heat generated by the body permitted to escape. These results can best be accomplished by having the clothes very loose fitting, so as to leave ample air space, and by having the outer clothes of a good non-conductor of heat. The cloth, of course, should be as light in weight as possible, but it is more important to have it a good non-conductor of heat and of porous weave.

Not enough attention is paid to the selection of colors[Pg 428] for resisting the heat. Two cloths identical except in color will show a great difference in the comparative amount of heat they let through. Light shades should be chosen, but care should be taken to see that they are not glaring, so as to irritate the eye and increase the mental effect of heat.

Linen and silk are better non-conductors than wool. And the weave of a cloth has a great deal to do with the amount of heat it lets through. Smooth, hard weaves absorb much less heat than fuzzy weaves. For this reason, serge is much cooler than worsted of the same shade and weight. A mistake is often made, however, in getting serge of a dark blue. It should be of as light a color as possible; gray is much cooler than blue. A white serge is much cooler than white flannel, because it is less fuzzy.

Linen is much cooler than woolens, because it is a better non-conductor and is of more porous weave. The linen thread is rough, which causes inequalities in the weave, permitting a more thorough circulation of air. Cotton is a still better non-conductor than linen, and would be preferable for summer clothes but for the fact that it neither wears nor holds its shape so well.

Mohair is very light in weight and cool looking. As a matter of fact, however, it is a fairly good conductor of heat, is closely woven, and usually comes in dark shades. It is a woolen cloth, and any woolen has its threads woven more closely on account of the process of manufacture than linens, cotton, and silk cloths. Linen is perhaps the best material for summer wear. It is porous in weave, light in color, and of fairly light weight.

It is well to remember that the safety valve of the body in hot weather is the evaporation of perspiration, not the act of perspiring. If the hand is put in a glove, for instance, it will perspire much more than if in the open air, but it will not be as cool. It is the evaporation that is a cooling process. If the perspiration is absorbed it cannot evaporate. That is why loose fitting undergarments are cooler than tight ones. It is also the reason why cotton is cooler next to the skin than linen or silk; it absorbs moisture less freely.

Drink Plenty of Water.—Water, and a great deal of[Pg 429] it, is desirable at any time during the summer. It should be drunk freely during the day. Lemonade also is good, the slight acid being an aid to digestion. It is best to have beverages cooled only to a moderate temperature. Ice water is not bad, but it would be preferable if it were not at so extreme a temperature. Ice is resorted to only as a convenient means of securing a palatable temperature; the system does not crave extreme cold. Water at the temperature of the air is nauseating, so ice is put into it and the other extreme secured. Sixty degrees is the ideal temperature for drinking water. If this could be conveniently obtained it would be preferred to a greater degree of cold. Not only is it less harmful to the system, but it is more satisfying and thirst-quenching. Water put in bottles and left in a refrigerator until properly chilled is the best way of preparing a summer beverage. When any beverage is sufficiently cold to cause a pain in the head or throat when drinking it the result may be harmful. Cold water poured on the wrist or head has a cooling effect and tends to reduce the ice water habit.

If one could afford it, it would be well to drink nothing but mineral water in the summer. Not only does it assure purity, but the gas is an aid to digestion and serves to render the water more palatable. This results in more of it being drunk than if it were flat water, and it is desirable to drink as much water as possible in hot weather. By mineral water I mean carbonated bottled waters intended for table use. Care should be taken that the water is only lightly impregnated with salt.

It is much safer to drink a well-known water. The water may not be bottled at the spring or it may be bottled under unsanitary conditions. In many cases mineral water is not all that it should be in cleanliness. Unless one is sure of the purity of a bottled water good hydrant water supplied through the city pipes is safer.

In traveling, however, and at summer resorts it would be well to drink nothing but mineral water of a well-known brand. Only by doing this and by being certain that the bottle has not been refilled can one be safe. The supplied on trains and in resorts frequently is not as pure as that supplied in large cities.[Pg 430]

On the whole, however, mineral water has no particular advantage over ordinary water except that the well-known brands are sure to be pure, and the carbonization makes it more tasty and so increases the amount consumed. It is much safer and more healthful to drink a well-known mineral water than the so-called soft drinks, many of which are unclean and harmful.

[Pg 431]

DISEASES OF WOMEN

[Pg 433]

CHAPTER XXIX

DISEASES OF WOMEN

Importance of Diseases of Women—The Beginning of Female Disease—Ailing Women Are Inefficient—As Home-makers, as Wife, as Mother—Few Ailing Women Become Pregnant—The Chief Cause of Female Disease—The Existence of the Average Mother—Female Diseases Are Avoidable—The Story of the Wife—Women Who Don't Want Children—Abuse of the Procreative Function—What the Woman with Female Disease Should Do—Cancer in Women—Cancer of the Breast—Cancer of the Womb—What Every Woman Should Know About Cancer—Change of Life—The Menopause—The Climacteric—The Average Age at Which the Change of Life Occurs—Symptoms of the Change of Life—Importance of a Correct Diagnosis—Danger Signals of the Change of Life—Conduct During the Change of Life.

No conscientious physician can give thought to this subject without being profoundly stirred. It may justly be said that all types of disease affecting the general health, the happiness, and the efficiency of the people are equally important, and should elicit the same degree and quality of kindly consideration. For many reasons this is not so, as I will endeavor to show. The dominating reason which renders diseases of women an exception to this rule may be mentioned here, however, so that the reader will keep its supreme significance prominently in mind while considering the subject in its various other aspects. "Diseases of women" rank first as a eugenic problem. They have a direct and far-reaching influence on posterity. They affect the environment of the home and thereby the health and the efficiency of all concerned.

The diseases which form the basis of the statements in this article are as follows: leucorrhea, displacements, or malpositions of the internal organs; lacerations, ulcers, tumors, sexual incompetency, and the venereal complications.[Pg 434]

It is not possible or desirable to tabulate the symptoms which result from these conditions. They would not convey to the average individual a just picture or an intelligent summary of the life of a victim of these ailments. An actual description of the life of a patient will be more effective because it will depict the incidental domestic atmosphere in which most of these patients live.

The Beginning of Female Disease.—When a woman first begins to feel the effects of so-called "female weakness" she is conscious of not feeling "fit." She wonders what the matter is. She may not have actual pain at this time, simply the consciousness that "she is not what she used to be." Her work seems harder and more tedious, she worries without cause, she begins the day with less energy and ambition than she used to, her disposition is more uneven, more irritable and she tires easier and is more willing to retire earlier than formerly. After a time she has more or less undefined pains. It may be an occasional headache, or backache, or she may have various severe neuralgic twinges. She gets nervous and moody; her appetite is not good and she is troubled with constipation. A little later, the general condition growing worse, her nervous system suffers most. So she drifts into neurasthenia and has fits of crying and periods of melancholia. She is more irritable, more impatient, more dissatisfied with herself, her family, and her friends. She loses faith in herself, in the future, and even in her religion, and she may contemplate self-destruction.

There are thousands and thousands of just such women in the world, and the pity is that many of them are mothers. It is surely self-evident that these women must be failures as efficient factors in many ways.

NEUROPATHIC ANCESTRY[C]

From a first glance at the chart it would appear that Daniel was an accidental case of feeble-mindedness. His progenitors were, however, decidedly neuropathic. The presence of apoplexy, paralysis, alcoholism in a family should be watched for with vigilance because of their possible effect upon the nervous system of the offspring.

Parents would do well to scrutinize the man who "led a fast life" before allowing him marry their daughter. The world would be shocked if it knew how many men with disease enter into conjugal relations. David's father had syphilis. David's feeble-mindedness was probably only one of the awful results.

[C] "Feeble-mindedness; Its Causes and Consequences," Goddard, The Macmillan Company.

[Pg 435]

AILING WOMEN ARE INEFFICIENT

First of All as Home-makers.—No woman can possibly be expected to successfully conduct a home if she is not enjoying a reasonable degree of good health. A home inefficiently supervised is an instrument for evil. It engenders discord and discontent, and it is lacking in the spirit which is essential to the cultivation of good-fellowship and which encourages harmony.

As Wife.—Most men resent the burden and the discomfort and the expense of an ailing wife, no matter how well-intentioned they may be. It is a failing of the male species to be cursed with the inability to understand any type of nervousness in a wife. Being inexplicable to him he attributes the symptoms to an evil imagination or to a bad disposition. He believes he is being imposed upon and proceeds to resent it. Many homes are rendered permanently miserable and unhappy by a failure to comprehend the real source of the trouble and to apply the remedy. Being inefficient as a home-maker the wife is not able to carry out her part as housekeeper. The home atmosphere is wrecked, the husband seeks comfort and congenial fellowship elsewhere. His efficiency is compromised and his earning capacity interfered with.

As Mother.—Anyone familiar with the exacting obligations and responsibilities of motherhood can well appreciate that normal health is an essential requisite to its successful consummation. The success of motherhood depends upon the proper exercise of many diversified qualities, and those in turn primarily depend upon an adequate degree of physical fitness, otherwise failure is certain to ensue. A woman, therefore, cannot exercise her function of motherhood if she is a neurasthenic.

Inasmuch as it has been proved that the regeneration of the race is dependent upon the maintenance of mentally and physically fit mothers, any condition that interferes with this standard is contrary to the eugenic requirement. Children sent out into the word unfit physically or morally are factors detrimental to the best interests of society and to their own progress and prosperity. A mother rendered incapable through sickness is, therefore, a menace to the home and to the eugenic promise.

Few Ailing Women Become Pregnant.—Nature fortunately seems to apprehend the true condition because few of these women become pregnant. This suggests an inquiry into the cause, or causes, underlying this unfortunate situation.

Are women responsible for these ailments?[Pg 436]

Most married women whose health is broken down by some disease peculiar to their sex refer the commencement of their suffering to a confinement or premature birth. The large majority of those women whose health is affected, because of some "female weakness," suffer from a displacement, or malposition of the internal organs, and as this condition is most frequently a product of maternity, there would seem to be some reasonable degree of justification for the assumption that the wrecked health is the result of a legitimate physiological act, and consequently a natural phenomenon. This is not, however, altogether true. A displacement is not, under any circumstances, a natural process. It is the result of causes which are avoidable. Most of them are the penalties imposed by nature because of the infraction of her laws. We will not consider those causes which have their beginning in wrong methods of dress or conduct during the years prior to maternity. Many such cases exist, but they are too few in number to justify consideration at this time. They are frequent enough, however, to suggest to mothers that it is always wise to keep a close watch over the tendencies and conduct of their daughters.

The Chief Cause of Female Diseases.—When a woman has given birth to a child her womb begins to contract and in a very brief space of time will resume its normal position, provided nothing interferes with the process. Nature will do exactly what is right if she is permitted to work in her own way. In another part of this book I have explained why it takes time for the recently pregnant womb to contract to its normal size. There is a 600 per cent. increase in volume to be got rid of by absorption. This takes time and nature can not be hurried without "taking chances." This is just where the "cause" exists which we have been looking for. Women do take chances.

Every woman should stay in bed for at least three weeks after confinement and should spend another three weeks convalescing before she assumes any domestic duty. This is a reasonable proposition when one considers the actual situation. There is an enormous amount[Pg 437] of readjustment to be undertaken, and there is no way of hastening this process. There is, however, a way to assist nature and to prevent mistakes. That way is to remain in bed a sufficient length of time to allow proper contraction of the womb. While the ligaments and muscles are still lax, to not undertake any muscular effort that will overtax or overstrain them,—a condition that favors displacement by weakening the support of the womb. A woman cannot understand why she should stay in bed when she feels well enough to get up. It is, however, unjust to censure the sex on this account. I am convinced the fault lies with the medical profession who do not take time to explain, in language which a woman may understand, the important reasons why they should stay longer in bed despite the fact that they do feel well.

The Existence of the Average Mother.—In considering this subject it is necessary to give some serious thought to the domestic and financial circumstances of the thousands and thousands of average mothers. Every observing, thinking person knows that the average mother's existence is more or less of a never-ending tragedy. Physically, mentally, and spiritually, they are victims of unalterable economic and social exigencies. They are compelled, because of ignorance, to live an unsanitary and unhygienic existence. The care of home and children, and maybe the unappreciative and inconsiderate attention of a careless and vindictive husband, add to the incidental worries,—fraying her nerves and disposition,—of the ordinary routine of a cheerless, hopeless life. Add to this experience the enormous drain of frequent child bearing upon her vitality, and we have a picture with which every physician is familiar.

Can such a woman possibly observe the essential rules of the hygiene of pregnancy? Has she the time and the means to build up her reserve energy and strength to competently undertake the duties of maternity or motherhood? Is she physically fit to give birth to a child? After it is all over can she devote the time to permit nature to do her share of the physical readjustment? Can she afford, or will she be permitted to remain[Pg 438] in bed long enough to allow conditions to be favorable to getting up without "taking a chance"? Inasmuch as her muscular tone is poor, her strength depleted, her vitality wasted, her ambition and hope at a low ebb, nature should be given a longer time, under the most favorable hygienic and domestic conditions, to help in the problem of readjustment, because her whole future, as an efficient machine, as wife, as mother, as home-maker, and as an economic individuality, is dependent upon how this crisis is met. This is the most important problem which an enlightened civilization has before it. It is the supreme eugenic task, and it is the most pressing and the most vital question for statesmen to solve. No man can deny that the permanency of the state is dependent upon the function of motherhood, yet motherhood is conducted by unskilled labor—labor, the quality of which no business would tolerate. We also know that the health of the workman has become an economic problem. Capital finds that labor is of better quality, and consequently more remunerative in every sense, if the environment is conducive to happiness and health. Yet motherhood, the most important labor in the world, upon which the very existence of the state depends, in addition to being performed by unskilled labor, is undertaken by physically unfit and frequently unwilling laborers, in an environment which is a disgrace to civilization and which cannot be duplicated in the whole realm of the brute world. This is the quality of labor, the products of which constitute the state.

If anyone is disposed to believe that this is an over-drawn picture, let him study the facts brought out in the recent patent medicine investigation. It was found that one small, unimportant, quack medical company had under treatment at one time (the day the government closed it up) 200,000 women, suffering exclusively from female diseases. How many similar cases must there be to support the large advertising concerns, whose tentacles reach to the remotest corners of the country and who limit their activity and cater to "diseases of women" only. Let him also give some thought to the fact that no specialty in the whole field of legitimate medical practice[Pg 439] has grown with such enormous strides, or is as remunerative to the ordinary physician as the department of "diseases of women."

Female Diseases Are Avoidable.—If, as has been asserted, the great majority of these ailments are traceable to causes which are avoidable, what is the remedy? In one word it is "Enlightenment." We must educate the ordinary mother who is so busy over her wash tubs and babies that she has no time to seek information upon subject which she doesn't even know exist, who does not even know how to feed her baby as well as the scrubbiest cat does her kitten, who does not know what eugenics means and is interested in it even less. We must stop limiting our talks to theorizing in clubs and societies. We must carry the tidings to the firesides of those hundreds of thousands of women who would listen and act, but who do not know what to do or how to correct their faults.

There is another feature of this subject which should be recalled in this connection. It has already been gone into in detail in the article on eugenics. There are many thousands of women who are compelled to fight the battle of life, upon whom an unjust disease has been grafted, which is sapping their strength and vitality, and which they do not appreciate or understand. Husbands infect wives unwittingly, wreck their constitutions, blast their hope of ever having a child, and then heap upon them abuse for an inability for which they are themselves directly responsible. Many homes are desecrated in this way and the real culprit is never suspected. Many women, who begin their married life under the most auspicious conditions so far as physical fitness or temperamental quality is concerned, have their health, and happiness, and success utterly ruined, and after spending a miserable, wretched existence, have their hope of maternity forever blasted on the operating table. The story of "the wife" has never been told. It is God's riddle.

Women Who Don't Want Children.—Sometimes the woman is at fault. Many young wives begin married life with the intention of not having a child for a year[Pg 440] or two. They don't want to be tied down too soon. They want some fun themselves. They are willing to become the legal mistress of a man, but they are not willing to assume the responsibilities of married life. It is difficult to understand the ethics of this type of morality. I have always given these young wives credit with simply not knowing what they were doing. Either their education or their common sense is lamentably deficient, or what is still worse, their mother was the wrong kind of a woman. If these unfortunate young wives have no regard for the cultivation of a good conscience, they should at least have some regard for their own health. From a purely selfish standpoint,—the standpoint of efficiency and success,—one would imagine these women would be unwilling to risk their whole future physical welfare on the chance of immunity—and it is a small chance.

Abuse of the Procreative Function.—In order to carry out this programme, various means are brought into requisition. In many cases I have known the wife has compelled the husband to wear devices which rendered conception impossible. This is a highly reprehensible procedure. If continued for any length of time it will seriously affect the husband's nervous system and general health, as this act is simply a form of self-abuse. Any husband who will tolerate such imposition is beginning married life wrong. He will pay a high price for his complacency. Any woman who suggests or acquiesces in such an arrangement is a moral degenerate and is absolutely unworthy of ever becoming a mother.

Some women buy expensive and fantastic syringes and proceed to abuse themselves with strong antiseptic solutions. This will result in killing the sensitiveness of the terminal nerves and end in depriving themselves of the pleasure with which a wise Providence endowed the procreative act. If the element of sexual incompetency enters the home of a young couple, it is the beginning of the end and each chapter of the story will be a worse hell than the one just ended. The wise husband will see that its cause will not be tolerated or begun in his family.[Pg 441]

If pregnancy should unwittingly occur they do not hesitate to adopt drastic means to "bring themselves around." They will procure some prescription which may have gone the rounds as a "marvel" but which always fortunately fails when they need it most. Thus they subject their system to the shock of violent medication and lay up for themselves in the future untold miseries. If these means fail, they go to "a woman whom they know" who "brings them around." If these young wives only knew what they were doing they could not be bought at any price to submit to such surgical tragedies. The least probable result will be that when the time arrives and circumstances are opportune to have a baby, and when it is their dearest wish to be a mother, they will discover that they no longer possess the ability to conceive. Many homes have been rendered childless in just this way. You cannot violate the laws of nature without paying the penalty in some way, and it is usually a sad reckoning.

What the Woman With Female Disease Should Do.—To those wives who are suffering with "female weakness," or who are in poor health without apparent or known cause, I would strongly advise a visit to their family physician or to an expert in diseases of women. Tell him exactly how you feel and submit to a thorough examination. Most of the diseases of women are readily curable, and if treated right all the symptoms which have rendered life miserable will disappear. It may be stated with the strongest emphasis, however, that no treatment from an advertising concern, or any patent medicine ever made, will in any sense cure any of these ailments. Every cent invested in any of these nostrums is money wasted. Medicine by the mouth is never necessary to affect a cure of the actual ailment. A physician will doubtless prescribe a tonic for your general rundown condition. But even this would totally fail if the cause of the ill health was not removed, and this necessitates an examination and special local treatment. For any advertising concern to assert that it can tell what ails a patient by simply filling out a symptom blank is utter nonsense. It is worse. It is obtaining money under[Pg 442] false pretenses, and should be punishable by imprisonment at hard labor for a long term.

CANCER IN WOMEN

My only object in referring to this disease is to direct the attention of women to its symptoms.

The only cure for cancer at the present time is the knife. If the disease can be reached it can be cured, if taken in hand early.

In women, cancer occurs most frequently in the breast and in the womb.

Cancer of the Breast.—Of all the tumors which affect the breast, cancer is the most frequent. Any tumor in the breast of a woman forty years of age or more is quite likely to be a cancer. A tumor (or lump) which has remained small for years and then begins to grow rapidly has changed its type and become cancerous. Many such tumors change in this way during the "change of life." Any tumor of the breast, at any age, which remains despite effort to dissipate it should be removed by operation. A physician is not justified in assuring a woman that a lump in the breast is harmless. It should be cut into and examined to positively decide its character. Early operation of tumors of the breast has greatly reduced the percentage of deaths from cancer.

Cancer of the Womb.—Occasional slight hemorrhages becoming more frequent, and later more abundant and offensive, constitute one of the first symptoms of cancer of the womb. Between the actual bleedings there is a discharge resembling dish-water. This discharge has a foul odor. Pain is as a rule a late symptom. Sometimes a severe pain extending into the hip or abdomen is an early symptom but it is very infrequent. Every woman over thirty who has a persistent leucorrhea, or any irregularity of the menstrual function, should be examined for cancer.

What Every Woman Should Know About Cancer.— Inasmuch as cancer is curable if taken early, every woman should take steps to be on the safe side.

If cancer is not taken early, it is certain death. A[Pg 443] very large number die who could have been saved.

Every lump in the breast should be positively diagnosed by cutting into it and examining it. It would be safer to remove every tumor of the breast at an early date.

Any discharge from the privates of a woman which has a bad or foul odor is suspicious; any irregular bleeding is more than suspicious. Any woman having these symptoms should be examined by a competent physician. Every woman over thirty-five years of age should be examined by a physician every six months. No woman should enter the change of life without a very thorough examination. Cancer is a disease which does not permit "taking a chance" with. It is far better to be certain, since it is curable if caught early, than to find out about it when too late, because, "too late" means death.

"CHANGE OF LIFE." THE MENOPAUSE

The average period of life during which a woman menstruates is from thirty to thirty-two years. When this period is about to expire she enters what is termed the "change of life," or the menopause, or the climacteric.

The average age at which "change of life" occurs in this country is about the forty-sixth year. It may normally occur, however, at any time between the fortieth and fiftieth year. There are cases on record when it has occurred earlier than the fortieth and later than the fiftieth year. When menstruation in a girl begins early, the menopause occurs late. On the other hand, if a girl does not have her regular monthly periods until she is older than usual,— about the eighteenth or twentieth year,—the "change of life" will set in at a very early age. Women who are victims of certain exhausting diseases, as, consumption, Bright's disease of the kidney, diabetes, or whose health is poor because of general physical debility from any cause, or who have had a large number of children in rapid succession, enter the "change of life" earlier than they otherwise would if their health was good. In women who are excessively fat the menopause is apt to occur at an early age. On[Pg 444] the other hand disease of the generative organs, or the presence of tumors of the womb may retard the process. Women in the higher walk of life, those living in cities those who do not labor or exercise sufficiently will enter this period at an earlier date than those who live in the country, who work and are physically more healthy.

Symptoms of "Change of Life."—When the menopause begins, the monthly periods are less profuse, the flow is scanty. As the months pass, menstruation becomes less and less until it ceases entirely. In a certain number of cases it stops abruptly and never appears again. Sometimes a period misses altogether, or a number of periods are passed over without any sign of menstruation, after which it may reappear either as a scanty flow, or as a profuse discharge. This may be followed for a number of months by irregular appearances of the menstrual phenomenon and then by its total cessation.

These may be the only symptoms or signs of the "change of life," and this is the normal state if the health is good. It cannot, however, be said that this is the average experience. Unfortunately the women of the present time do not live lives which conduce to robust health at this period of life. We find as a rule that the general health is below par. So they suffer from headache, "flushes," digestive disturbances, and many nervous symptoms which appear to be directly caused by the process through which they are passing. The "flushes" are disagreeable experiences. They consist of a feeling of heat which spreads over the entire body as if the blood was rushing to the surface and to the head. These flushes are followed by sweating and chilly sensations. The nervous symptoms may be quite marked. The woman loses her interest in the daily happenings. She may have mental vagaries, she is irritable and often melancholy and periods of seeming insanity may occur.

Importance of a Correct Diagnosis.—It is a mistake to attribute every symptom a woman may have at this time of life to the menopause. She is just as liable to develop conditions at this time, which she would at any age, and which have no relation to the "change of life." Every symptom should, therefore, be carefully investigated,[Pg 445] because serious conditions may complicate the menopause, and if attributed to it and neglected, may end disastrously.

During the "change of life," the generative organs become smaller or, as it has been termed, "dry up." The breasts also are involved in the shrinking process. It is quite a common experience for women to "lay on" fat, to become "flabby," at this age.

It is important that women should become familiar with the ordinary symptoms of the "change of life," in order that they may be constantly on guard against conditions that may indicate danger. Medical investigation has conclusively proved that many women lose their lives because they regarded the presence of certain symptoms as common to the "change of life." There is a tendency to disease at this time which must be intelligently considered, and if women are not posted to note unusual signs or symptoms they may neglect or ignore them, only to find when too late that these signs and symptoms were no part of the "change of life."

The Danger Signals of the Change of Life.—There are certain "danger signals" which should warn every woman that something is amiss, these are:—

(1) Profuse bleeding during the process of the "change."

(2) Bleeding occurring between the regular menstrual periods.

(3) The reappearance of slight bleedings or hemorrhages after menstruation has ceased for a number of months.

These symptoms are always suggestive of the presence of conditions that should not exist. They may indicate cancer, or some less serious condition that is amenable to cure by prompt and efficient treatment. Inasmuch as they may mean the beginning of cancer,—as explained in the preceding chapter on cancer, and which should be read in this connection,—immediate steps should be taken to find out the actual facts. Delay means death if it is cancer, while the most recent statistics show that in many cases a complete cure is possible if the surgeon gets the case early.[Pg 446]

Conduct During "Change of Life."—When a woman enters the "change of life" she is approaching a crisis that demands the most conscientious attention on her own part, and the sincerest consideration by all around her. She has reached the time of life when she owes herself something, and if she is wise she will willingly pay the debt. If she is not in good health she must make every effort to regain it promptly, even if radical measures must be employed in doing so. Nothing will contribute to her mental and physical comfort more than robust health during this period.

She must employ every hygienic measure that experience has taught us contributes to our well being. She must live an outdoor life as much as possible, taking sufficient exercise to keep the muscles and bodily functions in good condition. If she cannot exercise enough she should sit out of doors, dressed in seasonable clothing, and she should make up the deficiency in exercise by employing a competent masseuse. A thorough massage twice a week is sufficient. If her physician recommends an occasional Turkish bath it is a desirable aid as it helps the skin to throw off any excess of waste matter that may be circulating in the blood.

The home environment of these women should be congenial, and they should be relieved of the work and worry incident to domestic life. The nervous condition demands this degree of consideration, and the husband should make it his business to see that the wife, who has toiled to aid him during all the long years of married companionship, is accorded every possible help through the most trying and important period of her life. It is not to be understood, however, that she should be left without occupation. It is possible to indulge in congenial work which will occupy her time and attention without overtaxing her strength or fraying her nerves. A certain amount of amusement is desirable, and helps to tide over periods that might lag and encourage introspection and worry. An entire change of scenery and surroundings. A visit to the seashore or to the mountains is to be commended.

During this period the diet should be simple and the[Pg 447] bowels should be kept open regularly. Inasmuch as these patients frequently suffer from digestive disturbances, it is wise to refrain from those articles of diet that ordinarily cause indigestion. Such articles are, sweet dishes, pies, pastries, candies, fresh bread, fried food, sugars, and the relishes and seasoning extras which constitute the et ceteras of the table. Meat should never be taken to excess, alcohol and all stimulants are to be avoided. Water may be taken freely to advantage.

[Pg 449]

THE PATENT MEDICINE EVIL

[Pg 451]

CHAPTER XXX

THE PATENT MEDICINE EVIL

What Mothers Should Know About the Patent Medicine Evil—Tonics—Used by Temperance People Because it Could "Stimulate"—Stomach Bitters—Blood Bitters—Sarsaparilla—Celery Compounds—Malt Whisky—Headache Remedies—Pain Powders—Anti-headache Powders—Headache Powders—Soothing Syrups—Baby's Friends—Catarrh Powders—Kidney Pills—Expectorant—Cough Syrup—Lithia Waters—Health, Wealth and Happiness for a Dollar a Bottle—New Discovery for Consumption—Consumption Cure—Cancer Cures—Pills for Pale People—Elixir of Life.

WHAT MOTHERS SHOULD KNOW ABOUT THE PATENT MEDICINE EVIL

Much has been written about the patent medicine evil during the past few years. One very thorough crusade has been instituted and efficiently carried through, exposing the evils of the patent medicine business. Whatever legislation is in force to-day which has for its object the regulation of the evil, is largely a product of that crusade. Notwithstanding these efforts, it is a fact that scarcely any of the great majority who should be interested in the subject, because they are its victims, have any knowledge of the nature or extent of the evil, or appreciate its far-reaching and pernicious influence. For two reasons I regard it as peculiarly fitting, that the subject should be given adequate consideration in this book:—

First, because mothers should be told the whole truth about all conditions that have any influence on the health of the members of the home.

Second, because though we are the victims of many evils and many forms of "graft," which directly or indirectly[Pg 452] affect our pockets and our morals, we submit to them because they have no bearing on the physical well-being of the race. As mothers, however, and as the conservers of the fitness of the family and the home, we are directly and rightly interested in an evil which deeply affects the health and the efficiency of members of the family as the patent medicine evil does. It is through the mothers of the race that this enemy of the home must be finally and completely overthrown. If every mother in the land could be taught to understand even a fraction of the truth of the insidious wrong hidden under the mask of the nostrum advertisement, we would witness a righteous resentment that could only be satisfied by legislative enactment that would wipe out forever the whole infamous business. No spasmodic or localized effort will ever succeed against this public enemy. Its very strength is the people whom it dupes and despises, because they supply the money with which the patent medicine combine fights its battles.

It has been estimated that three hundred millions of dollars are spent annually on patent medicines and fake medical cures in the United States. Three hundred million dollars fraudulently obtained every year, mostly from the poor, is surely a subject deserving of honest and careful consideration.

The pure food and drug act compelled the manufacturers of patent medicines to publish the formulæ of their remedies on their labels. This is a big step in the right direction. Many States have helped the propaganda in one way or another, but much remains to be done. When the formulæ were demanded it was discovered that all nostrums belonged to a certain class. For example it was found that the soothing syrups—which are fed to babies—all contained opium in some form, or an equally dangerous drug. The headache remedies were all dangerous, every one of them containing ingredients which affect the heart seriously. The so-called tonics owed their chief virtue to their stimulating effect, which was due to the alcohol they contained and which in many instances practically equaled ordinary whisky in quality, quantity, and effect.[Pg 453]

It has been authoritatively stated that more alcohol is consumed in this country in patent medicines than is dispensed in a legal way by licensed liquor venders, barring the sale of ales and beer.

Many so-called remedies were found to contain absolutely no medication at all. They were simply sugar, or starch, or some harmless substance. But they were being sold to cure anything from kidney disease to cancer. It was an astonishing revelation and in a way it showed how far men will go to attain financial success.

A well-known tonic was at the time of the investigation one of the most prominent proprietary nostrums in the country. The actual cost including bottle, label, contents, and packing is between fifteen and eighteen cents. It costs in the drug store $1.00 per bottle. It was found to contain alcohol and water and a pinch of burnt sugar for coloring purposes, and one-half of one per cent. of mild drugs. It was claimed that it would cure all or any of the diseases listed in the book, and that list practically includes all the ills of man. It is within the limits of truth to assert that this tonic, though advertised as a medicine, was largely in demand as a stimulant and intoxicant,—just as a certain famous malt whisky is to-day. Voluminous evidence is on record wherein it is shown that it was used in enormous quantities as a stimulant, in exactly the same way as ordinary whisky is used. The dose of any medicine is, as a rule, seldom over a tablespoonful three or four times a day. The average individual would imagine that there would be some risk attached to increasing the dose from a tablespoonful to the contents of a large size bottle. The only risk was that the patient got a more profound and maybe a more satisfying "jag." In "no license" towns this tonic was bought by the druggists in gross lots and used exclusively for its intoxicating properties. In southern Ohio, and in the mountain districts of West Virginia the "—— jag" was a standard form of intoxication. In many Southern newspapers there appeared regularly advertised cures for the "—— habit," brought on by the use of this preparation,—and no doubt the cure was a stronger percentage of liquor as this scheme was frequently[Pg 454] worked to steal the patients from one remedy to another.

The following communication was sent out by the Department of the Interior, as a result of the alarming reports which were regularly reaching Washington regarding the prevalence of drunkenness among the Indians, despite the fact that "no liquor" was sold in these government reservations. The fact was that the Indians had discovered this pleasant tonic.

DEPARTMENT OF THE INTERIOR
Office of Indian Affairs.
Washington, D. C.
To Indian Agents and School Superintendents in charge of Agencies:

In connection with this investigation, please give particular attention to the proprietary medicines and other compounds which the traders keep in stock, with special reference to the liability of their misuse by Indians on account of the alcohol which they contain. The sale of ——, which is on the lists of several traders, is hereby absolutely prohibited. As a medicine, something else can be substituted; as an intoxicant, it has been found too tempting and effective....

Mr. S. H. Adams in "The Great American Fraud" writes as follows: "The other reason why this or some other of its class is often the agency of drunkenness instead of whisky is that the drinker of it doesn't want to get drunk, at least she doesn't know that she wants to get drunk. I use the feminine pronoun advisedly, because the remedies of this class are largely supported by women. Several of the others of these well-known proprietary medicines depend for their popularity chiefly on their alcohol. One celery compound relieves depression and lack of vitality on the same principle that a cocktail does, and with the same necessity for repetition. I know an estimable lady from the Middle West who visited her dissipated brother in New York— dissipated from her point of view, because she was a pillar of the W. C. T. U., and he frequently took a cocktail before dinner and came back with it on his breath, whereon she would weep over[Pg 455] him as one lost to hope. One day, in a mood of brutal exasperation, when he had not had his drink and was able to discern the flavor of her grief, he turned on her: 'I'll tell you what's the matter with you,' he said, 'You're drunk—maudlin drunk!'

"She promptly and properly went into hysterics. The physician who attended diagnosed the case more politely, but to the same effect, and ascertained that she had consumed something like half a bottle of a certain swamp root that afternoon. Now, swamp root is a very creditable 'booze,' but much weaker in alcohol than most of its class. The brother was greatly amused until he discovered, to his alarm, that his drink abhorring sister couldn't get along without her patent medicine bottle! She was in a fair way, quite innocently, of becoming a drunkard."

Another famous stomach bitters was found to contain, according to an official State analysis, 44 per cent. of alcohol; another mixture contained 20 per cent. of alcohol; a certain blood bitters contained 25 per cent. of alcohol; a sarsaparilla 26 per cent.; a celery compound 21 per cent.; the malt whiskey is in this class and is a particularly obnoxious fraud, for it pretends to be a medicine and to relieve all kinds of lung and throat disease. It is especially favored by temperance people because in this way they get their "grog" in the guise of a medicine. It is sold in many places across the bar of saloons at 15 cents per drink, as many other brands of rye and Bourbon whisky are sold.

Think of treating any disease of the stomach with the famous stomach bitters containing 44 per cent. of alcohol,—just 6 per cent. less than the amount of alcohol in an ordinary bottle of whisky. Yet all of these patent medicines have made fortunes for their owners, some of them have made millions in a few years.

A number of years ago a company with a keen vision for profits conceived the idea of bottling the water of the Great Lakes and selling it at almost champagne prices. When delivered to the druggist ready for sale the "remedy" contained 99 per cent. water, the other 1 per cent. consisting of a few drops of an inert acid, used simply[Pg 456] to give it a slight tart taste. The preparation had absolutely no medical utility of any description.

One of the greatest advertising crusades ever carried out in the interest of a patent medicine was inaugurated and in these advertisements it was claimed that it would cure:—

Asthma, Bronchitis, Coughs, Colds, Cancer, Dyspepsia, Fevers, Hay Fever, Leucorrhea, Piles, Quinsy, Skin Diseases, Throat Troubles, Abscess, Blood Poison, Consumption, Catarrh, Dandruff, Gallstones, Influenza, Malaria, Rheumatism, Tuberculosis, Anemia, Bowel Troubles, Contagious Diseases, Dysentery, Diarrhea, Eczema, Erysipelas, Goiter, Gout, La Grippe, Neuralgia, Scrofula, Tumors, Ulcers,

all diseases that begin with fever, inflammations, all catarrh, all contagious diseases, all the results of impure or poisoned blood. "In nervous diseases this remedy acts as a vitalizer, accomplishing what no drugs can do." These are the exact words of the advertisement. It ought to take a stronger vitalizer than water from the Great Lakes to induce anyone to believe such a story; and yet this company attained a remarkable success and had no difficulty in obtaining thousands of testimonials.

We are certainly a nation of dupes, and Barnum's dictum, that "the public loves to be fooled," is literally true. In a number of instances the proprietor of a successful remedy has been asked under oath if his preparation had any curative value and he has refused to answer the question, while thousands of foolish people have sent him unsolicited testimonials asserting its remarkable merits as a cure in all kinds of conditions. Some of these ignorant people actually believe what they write, but most of them[Pg 457] write "to see their name in the paper," while many of them are paid for it.

It was stated in the literature sent all over the country by this company that their remedy was really liquid oxygen. It would be nearer the truth to state that the moon was made of green cheese. The one assertion can be disproved, the other cannot with scientific exactness. Liquid oxygen practically does not exist. Assuming that it could be obtained in teaspoonful doses, and assuming that some dauntless individual made the attempt to take a dose, he would never swallow it for the reason that it would freeze his teeth, tongue, mouth, and throat, so that they would be useless to him for the remainder of his life. If by any miracle it could be swallowed, the undertaker would have to thaw him out over a stove in order to assure him a respectable burial. We may safely feel certain that the nostrum was not liquid oxygen. It is, however, a very fair sample of the foolish kind of lies which all of these nostrum venders employ,—they are after, and appeal only to the ignorant. I am informed that the directors of this company decided to retire as ordinary millionaires rather than risk the chance of developing nervous prostration, in which event they might have felt it somewhat disloyal not to have taken their own medicine.

Headache Remedies.—Most headache remedies are dangerous. The following are in this class; orange powders, bromo powders, pain powders, headache powders, anti-headache, and practically all headache powders or remedies sold in drug stores.

Many deaths are on record from the use of orange powders and from others. There are many examples of what an unthinking individual may do to helpless little children.

Orange powders were recommended for the cure of asthma, biliousness, headache, colds, catarrh, grip, diarrhea, hay fever, insomnia, neuralgia, seasickness, and sciatica. There is no known cure for a number of these diseases, and apart from the malicious assumption of the claim, orange powders will not cure any of them.

Another dangerous headache nostrum, widely advertised all over the country, is responsible for many deaths[Pg 458] as a result of its use. It is absolutely unsafe, as previously stated, to use any of these remedies. Death by heart failure is on the increase in this country and it may safely be attributed to the indiscriminate use of these powerful and toxic nostrums.

The "soothing syrups" depend upon opium to effect their result. The drugging of helpless infants has been a source of profit to the vender of patent medicines for many years. A certain Baby Friend,—a touching name, and in which one would not expect to find an enemy in the guise of a deadly poison,—is a combination of sweetened water and morphine. This disgraceful mixture, considering the use for which it was designed, would be bad enough if it was the evil concoction of a man rendered irresponsible by a strenuous craving for blood-money, but to know that its proprietor is a woman seems beyond belief. I wonder if she would feel sufficiently respectable and decently clean enough to stand on the platform and face an audience of American mothers? I think not.

Catarrh powders contain, as a rule, cocaine, one of the most insidious and dangerous of drugs. None of them cure catarrh, they simply relieve for the time being at the expense of injuring more vital parts. Their use also very frequently disposes the victim to postpone treatment that would be beneficial until too late. M——'s Kidney Pills were said to cure Bright's disease, gravel, all urinary troubles and pain in the back or groins from kidney disease. Analysis showed them to consist of ordinary white sugar. They contained absolutely no medication, and yet they were freely sold to cure the above serious conditions. A famous expectorant and an equally famous cough syrup contain opium and when taken for the cure of cough are distinctly dangerous.

It is foolish and unnecessary to name any other patent medicine in the list of those that are distinctly harmful and dangerous to use. There are hundreds of them. It would take a book of a thousand pages to give their names and write the data that have been obtained against them. Every advertised medicine should be absolutely avoided. I could fill this book with the death certificates of those[Pg 459] who have died as a result of the indiscriminate use of advertised nostrums. It is an appalling record; the unfortunate part being that it is impossible to acquaint every citizen with the facts.

Duplicity and misrepresentation are not confined to patent medicines. Even the mineral waters are misrepresented and lied about. A much-advertised lithia water, before the passage of the pure food and drugs act, was highly vaunted as a uric acid eliminant because of the lithia it was said to contain. Thousands, probably millions of gallons of it have been sold during the past twenty years, to people who could not very well afford to pay for it, because of this claim, despite the fact that it is well known that lithia is not a uric acid eliminant, and despite the additional important fact that the government analysis of this lithia water proved that it practically contained no lithia whatsoever. It is now being sold as an "alkaline diuretic." This claim is no better supported by facts than the former claim that it was a lithia water. Of course it is a diuretic, because water is the best diuretic we possess, but any ordinary pure water, which costs nothing, will just as effectually accomplish all that this lithia water could as a diuretic.

It is a fact that the judgment of a sick person is not reliable. For this reason a physician never tries to treat himself when sick, nor will a physician treat any member of his family for much the same reason. His sentiment overrules his judgment and he cannot depend upon his decisions. An individual who is not well may be influenced by an irresponsible person, or by a clever, subtly worded advertisement, to use remedies that are not only dangerous in themselves, but which are wholly unsuited to the condition for which they are taken.

Quite a common characteristic of sick people is unreasonableness. They become irritable and discouraged, and not being able to rely upon their own judgment they fail to render to themselves the degree of justice that is essential to peace of mind and a favorable convalescence. They may place themselves in the care of a reputable and thoroughly qualified physician, but if they do not observe distinct evidences of improvement within a very[Pg 460] brief period they lose faith in him and change their doctor. They may do this a number of times, until finally they reach the conclusion that the entire medical profession is a fraud. They are then the legitimate victims of the patent medicine shark or the fake-curist. Probably ninety-nine per cent. of the victims of these parasites are obtained in this way. The statement often seen in testimonials to the effect, that "the best doctors failed to cure me," is not true in any instance. The truth is, that the individual failed to give the doctors the opportunity to cure him, and the reason he did not give them the chance was because they treated him as a man and as a human being, which he proved not to be. Had the first doctor he consulted adopted the tactics of the quack he would have cured him in a much shorter time. Instead of doing that, he told him the exact truth and charged him an ordinary office fee, while the quack told him lies and charged him a large sum of money to cure him. The latter gentleman, knowing the tendency to vacillate which these individuals have, ensured himself the time necessary to a cure by compelling him to pay the entire sum in advance, which is their universal custom. The patient, therefore, could not afford to change his doctor this time, and as time was all that was necessary to his cure, the wily and oily quack gets all the credit for effecting a cure, which "the best doctors could not accomplish." It is a simple game, and the explanation is just as simple, but there are those who will not see, and there are those who cannot be told.

It is not simple justice, however, to blame these individuals altogether. We must keep in mind the irresolute judgment which is to a certain extent a product of the ill-health with which the patient suffers and the consequent easy tendency to be persuaded one way or another. The way in which these people are influenced is always the wrong way for the following reason. No person with any judgment or common sense or justice or sympathy would be fool enough or inhuman enough to give advice to a suffering sick man or woman as to what he or she should do or take. These individuals do not lack advice, however. There is always the pestering idiot around[Pg 461] who knows exactly what should be done, and who does not hesitate to enter where an angel would fear to tread.

In the columns of almost every newspaper one may find promises of health, wealth and happiness for a dollar a bottle. Even consumption has been vaunted as an easily curable disease by a hundred different nostrums, though the truth is that it is incurable by any known drug. Men who advertise these remedies are deliberately trafficking in human life, and they are thoroughly well aware of it. It is difficult to conceive of the type of manhood who would advertise a remedy as "The only sure cure for consumption in the world;" this was extensively done by the concern that put a certain "New Discovery for Consumption" on the market. Further announcement was made that "it strikes terror to the doctors," and that it was "the greatest discovery of the century." Every such assertion is a lie. It was found to be a mixture of morphine and chloroform. It is a wicked concoction to give to any human being in good health. To a consumptive it is admirably designed to shorten the life of anyone who will take it steadily in the hope of a cure. It certainly struck terror in the hearts of the doctors after its composition was known and when it was remembered to whom it was to be given.

"Consumption Cure" was found to contain one of the most deadly of known poisons,—prussic acid. In a booklet which was sent out by the proprietors of a certain cough syrup the following contemptible assertion is made: "There is no case of hoarseness, cough, asthma, bronchitis, or consumption that cannot be cured speedily by the proper use of this cough syrup." Such a cruel and dangerously fraudulent statement is absolutely inexplicable to any honest mind. Dr. ——'s ---- pills for pale people, were advertised to cure paralysis. They were found to be made of green vitriol, starch and sugar.

Those who bought these nostrums not only wasted their money, but they threw away any chance of relief they have, by failing to adopt the proper treatment until it was too late.

In directing the attention of mothers to the evil of the patent medicine business it is my earnest hope that they[Pg 462] will give to the subject something more than a mere passing interest. To an intelligent individual no lengthy argument,—other than the recital of such facts as are given in this article,—is necessary to prove that it is an evil which is deserving of the most serious consideration.

The business is one that appeals only to the ignorant. This is a plain and probably a harsh assertion, nevertheless it is absolutely the simple truth. The language and the reasoning of the nostrum vender are not designed to appeal to the trained, educated mind, or to an individual possessing innate common sense. Even though the average person is unacquainted with the constituents of a remedy that apparently enjoys a large success, the absurd claims made for it should safeguard them against its use. Few would have purchased ordinary water at $1.00 a bottle had they known what they were buying. But an individual with any reasoning ability or ordinary common sense, should have been sceptical regarding the merits of any remedy that was claimed to "cure," among other diseases, consumption, cancer, rheumatism, malaria, gallstones, asthma, blood poison, dandruff, and all contagious diseases. It would be impossible to conceive a more mendacious and absurd claim, and it would be impossible to concoct a more impertinently foolish assumption than to assume that such a claim would receive the consideration of a sane mind.

Unfortunately, however, we are compelled to recognize that there are some curious people in the world, people whose reasoning methods are inexplicable, whose conclusions are not based upon any system of ethics or of logic. They believe what they choose to believe, irrespective of the quality of the testimony which may be advanced to refute their belief. The following incident illustrates this peculiar perversity: A woman patient of mine suffered from an obstinate and harassing cough. Though her general health was rather poor, her lungs were not affected. The cough persisted in spite of all efforts of specialists to alleviate it. The nervous condition of the patient, and an unusually long spell of inclement March weather, were directly responsible for the intractable character of the ailment. I advised her to[Pg 463] visit Florida. This advice was given because her parents were then residing in that State. She did go to Florida and her husband informed me a few weeks later that she was entirely free from the cough and was enjoying good health. A number of months later, shortly after her return home, I was called to attend her husband. During the conversation incident to the call, she asked if I "knew what cured her awful cough." Somewhat amazed, I replied, "Certainly, Florida." She answered, with positive emphasis, "No, sir, Florida did not." I then asked her to please explain the mystery and was regaled with the following interesting information:

A few days after she reached Florida she met a woman—one of those irresponsible individuals who meander through life giving free advice upon subjects which they know nothing about, who talk eruptively and voluminously because talking is an easily acquired habit. This particular missionary of evil immediately confided to her the secret of her life, how she was made a well woman and cured wholly of all physical ills. She told her there was a man in Kansas who had discovered a liquid, which, if dropped into the eye twice daily, would cure any disease afflicting any member of the human family. This exuberant spider induced her victim to enter her parlor where she convinced her at her leisure that she was preaching the gospel. The result was that our friend sent to Kansas for the "Elixir of Life." Meantime the climate of Florida was doing its work. But just at this psychological moment the "elixir" arrived. Two drops of the precious liquid were, with due solemnity and deliberation, instilled into her eye and in a few days her cough began to mend.

It would have been waste of time to have asked if she really believed the drops to be responsible for her cure. She spoke with the enthusiastic conviction of a disciple of a worthier cause. I inquired if she possessed any literature explaining the method of cure, and she presented me with the printed matter which is sent with the bottle. I told her I would look it over and tell her what I thought of it later.

The *Message of Facts*, which was the title of the newspaper, (it was printed like a newspaper and of the size[Pg 464] of an ordinary paper), contained complete information regarding the "wonderful remedy" and its discoverer. He assumed the title of Professor and candidly admitted that he had been arrested a number of times for practicing medicine without a license. He asserted that the reason of his numerous arrests was because the medical profession in the State of Kansas, being jealous of his success instigated a course of insistent persecution against him. He further asserted that he offered to sell his discovery to the State, but the State refused to purchase it, consequently he had to go on practicing to earn a living. With reference to his method of treatment he stated:

"Despite the fact that medical men are too unfair and too prejudiced to accord Professor —— the credit he has justly earned, there is no getting away from the plain truth, that the great scientist has originated a method of conquering human ills that has completely revolutionized the long-cherished theories of the medical schools."

And further, "... being the discoverer of my system and the only man in the world practicing it, and having all cures and no cases of injury as my record shows ..."

Note that, in the first quotation, he asserts that his methods have revolutionized the old-time theories. This would surely imply that the medical schools, having been compelled to note his successful ways, were compelled likewise to change their theories and teach his way of curing disease. Despite this strong and robust assertion he states, in the second quotation, that he is the only man in the world practicing his methods. Evidently he did not revolutionize to any very great extent.

He claimed to be able to cure any human ill, and particularly emphasized his ability to cure consumption, Bright's disease, diabetes, epilepsy, asthma, stomach troubles, nervous prostration, blindness, female diseases, paralysis, heart and kidney diseases.

He, of course, does not state the nature of his remedy. It consists of a liquid which is dropped into the eye, and the procedure is the same, no matter what disease afflicts the patient. It is not essential to write at length his explanation of the way in which this "marvelous discovery"[Pg 465] effects its cures. Suffice it to say, that it is a tissue of anatomical and physiological misrepresentation. He admittedly is uneducated and possesses absolutely no knowledge of even elementary medicine. His explanation is, therefore, to a medical mind, a ludicrous and an absurd attempt to tell what he does not understand. Of course, his explanation is not supposed to fall into the hands of a physician, and to a lay person, who understands as little as he does, it sounds all right. We must again fall back on the foolish claims he makes and on the basis of common sense we fail to understand how anyone can believe such stuff. Yet the woman who firmly believes that her cough was cured by this man has enthusiastically recommended the nostrum to a number of other women who have various ailments, all of whom are using it under her experienced instructions.

This is a very good illustration of how these impostors and charlatans succeed. This woman was approached at the psychological moment and was influenced to buy. It did not necessarily have to be these drops. It might just as well have been any other patent medicine, or any fake cure. It would have worked just the same for the reason that it was the climate of Florida that did the work. It is absurd to devote time even to consider the probability of the drops having aided in the cure. This man's whole scheme is a fake, pure and simple. No part of it has any merit. In other words, his remedy is no remedy at all, it is simply the mildest, ordinary eye wash, which may be bought in any drug store for ten cents. He charges $5.00, but think of the story he writes, think of the promises he gives and the claims he makes, and the paper he prints,—these all cost money and time and labor, and you must pay for them. And I know a woman who is putting these drops in her eye twice daily in the hope of correcting a displaced womb. Could the brain of the most facile weaver of romance conceive a more utterly absurd and pitiful condition of affairs than that an adult human being should be guilty of doing what an intelligent ant would not do under any circumstances?

When the "professor" claims that he refuses to "give up" his secret unless the State of Kansas adequately remunerates[Pg 466] him for it, which, of course, it rightly refuses to do—he demonstrates how absolutely devoid of horse sense he is. No man with a "cure" for consumption—without mentioning the many other equally remunerative "cures" which this wizard owns, and which may be appended to the consumption "cure" just as the side-shows journey in the wake of the big circus— need waste his precious time dickering with the unappreciative State of Kansas. If his "cure" is anywhere near twenty-four carat gold he can own the State of Kansas and he may add another one to it for good measure. Any man capable of doing one-thousandth part of what this wily "professor" claims to be able to do, would make so much money that it would embarrass him all the rest of his life. One of his claims is that he can cure epilepsy. If he could cure epilepsy he wouldn't be allowed to stay twenty-four hours in the State of Kansas. Every civilized country on the face of the earth would bid for his services as an economic necessity because as an investment he would be cheap at any price.

[Pg 467]

CHAPTER XXXI

THE PATENT MEDICINE EVIL—Continued

The —— Consumption Cure—Personals to Consumptives—Nature's Creation—Female Weakness Cures—Various Compounds and Malt Whiskies.

FRAUDULENT TESTIMONIALS

It would indeed seem to be an act of supererogation to compile further evidence of the infamy of this entire business: what additional proof is necessary?

A certain Dr. H. of ——, Mich., published widely the following advertisement:

"Gains 17 Pounds After Every One Gave Her Up.

"Miss I—— S—— had a terrible case of consumption, together with catarrh and bronchitis. With this terrible complication, given up to die, she took the H—— treatment. She is now cured."

Dear Doctor: I have been gaining rapidly. Have gained 17 pounds; weigh 150 pounds now and am getting quite strong, too. I wish you could see me. You would be surprised. I look just fine. Everybody says they never thought I would get well. I can't thank you enough for it. I am feeling just fine, so I will close.

Yours truly,

Miss I—— S——.

The above testimonial reads quite convincing and doubtless was the means of influencing many other unfortunate victims to put themselves under the "professional" care of Dr. H——. Investigation, however, revealed the fact that this optimistic young lady died shortly after giving the testimonial and that her death was, according to the transcript of her certificate of death issued by the State of Wisconsin, due to "consumption." The testimonial therefore cannot possibly have any value under the circumstances. Unfortunately, however, this doctor does not publish the death certificate with the[Pg 468] testimonial, which latter he continued to use after her death.

After an exhaustive inquiry into the personality and business of the above mentioned M. D., the *Journal of the American Medical Association* said:

First. The H—— consumption cure is chiefly owned and controlled by men whose only qualification for treating disease is that they are business men financially interested in other medical fakes.

Second. The claims made in the advertisements, either directly or by implication, that these "rcmedies" will "cure" consumption are cruel and heartless falsehoods.

Third. The methods employed to capture victims, by means of speciously worded circular letters disguised as personal communications, are an imposition, if not an actual fraud, on the ignorant and credulous.

Fourth. The drugs sent out by this concern as a "trial treatment" are worthless as a cure for consumption.

Fifth. In printing endorsements of himself, which this M.D. received from ministers of the gospel, he grossly abused the confidence of men who did not know the use to which their letters were to be put.

Sixth. The testimonials from physicians which he publishes have been shown to emanate in some cases from men who themselves are employed in exploiting medical fakes.

Seventh. The claim he makes of being a graduate of Edinburgh University has been shown to be as false as the claims made for the nostrum he exploits.

Can a much more disgraceful business than the various "consumption cure" humbugs be imagined? Founded on fraud, maintained by deceit, perpetuated by falsehood—the sick are exploited to pay dividends on corporate quackery. How much longer will this outrage on the unfortunate victims of the White Plague be tolerated? If not for humanitarian reasons, then for its own protection, at least, society should demand that such cruel frauds be suppressed. Their existence is a menace to public health and a disgrace to modern civilization.

Many fraudulent nostrums are advertised as blind advertisements in the "Personal" columns of the daily press. The following recently appeared in the "Personal" columns of papers all over the country:

PERSONAL—TO CONSUMPTIVES: I possess information which cost me a fortune, and feel that I should let every consumptive know about my experience. Mrs. R., Ohio.

[Pg 469]

To those who answered this advertisement was sent a letter written on pale blue stationery, such as is used for social correspondence, with the initials —. R. embossed, monogram style, in gilt on the paper and envelope, signed "Mrs. —. R." It is asserted in this letter that the writer has cured herself "in defiance of the world's scientists," by the discovery of "a combination of certain roots and herbs." As a consequence of having made this discovery, and after spending a fortune in the quest of a cure according to the advertisement, we are informed that "I am now devoting my life to saving others." According to further information, her effort is apparently successful, because she "finds it impossible to attend personally to the multitude of inquiries with which she is favored." She finds it necessary, therefore, "to refer your letter to my secretary, Mr. C——, from whom you will no doubt hear soon." The secretary is very evidently on the job, "for in the next mail there is delivered a letter from the —— Company, signed H. W. C——, Sec'y."

We can estimate the degree of Mrs. R.'s solicitude for the welfare of the race when we learn that the same concern was engaged in exploiting a syphilis "cure" in Chicago a few years ago. In all probability the cure is the same for both diseases. It is difficult to tell of which disease it was that Mrs. R. cured herself.

Among the testimonials published by this concern in its booklet are quite a number in which the statement is made, frequently in glowing terms, that the writer has been "cured" of consumption by ——. A few of these were investigated and in every instance the writer died of consumption. This mixture is, in the strongest terms that can be used, a fake, a fraud, and is not a "cure" for consumption, as, of course, every intelligent person knows.

TO CONSUMPTIVES.

The undersigned having been restored to health by simple means, after suffering for several years with a severe lung affection, and that dread disease Consumption, is anxious to make known to his fellow sufferers the means of cure. To those who desire it, he will cheerfully send (free of charge),[Pg 470] a copy of the prescription used, which they will find a sure cure for Consumption, Asthma, Catarrh, Bronchitis, and all throat and lung maladies. He hopes all sufferers will try his remedy, as it is invaluable. Those desiring the prescription which will cost them nothing, and may prove a blessing, will please address Rev. —— W., ——, N. Y.

A reply to this advertisement brought the information that the Rev. W—— contracted tuberculosis while in charge of a church in Maine, and after trying various treatments was finally cured by "a famous Dr. C——, of Paris, France." It was now his intention to "devote his life" to aid suffering humanity, in a spirit of thankfulness, by giving away, free of all charge, a copy of the famous prescription.

Investigation proved that the Rev. E. A. W—— did not exist, consequently he never had a church in Maine, nor did he contract tuberculosis, or consult Dr. C——, of Paris. The individual who conducted the business was really one C. A. A——, who, it is to be inferred, conceived the whole fake. The scheme was a simple one. When the prescription was received it was discovered that the ingredients were not known to the drug trade and it was necessary to send to Mr. A—— for a supply before it could be tested. The literature sent with the prescription was of such a character that the average ignorant sufferer from consumption, hoping against hope for a "cure," fell into the trap and sent the money for a trial shipment.

"FEMALE WEAKNESS" CURES

Dr. D——'s "—— Compound": This nostrum is sold to relieve the pain of child-birth. It is surely not necessary to state that it will not relieve the pains of child-birth, nor will any drug or drugs ever do so. The irresponsible group of quacks who claim to have solved the problem of "painless child-birth" through the use of various "compound's" hardly merit the consideration of ordinary individuals. It is almost impossible to believe that a man would print over his name such a puerile or fantastic story as the following. Dr. D—— asserts that the value of his compound is proved because a certain woman patient tells how, after losing her first child, she[Pg 471] had a vision. A "white-robed angel" appeared, who, after speaking to her in beautiful language, said, "Go, sister, and seek freedom and peace in the use of —— Compound and in following the teachings of that book."

The book is entitled "Painless Child-Birth," it sells for $2.00 and it simply extols, in unnecessary flowery language, the merits of the compound.

If we heard such stories in every-day life we would smile credulously at our informant and doubt his sanity, but in a patent medicine advertisement we expect to read of miracles and we almost hope to be told of impossible happenings. The more glaringly false and silly they seem to be, the more they seem to exert their subtle hypnotic influence on anyone whose physical or mental temperament lends itself to the appeal.

This compound "speedily cures all derangements and irregularities of the menstrual function, congestion, inflammation, ulceration and displacement of the womb, and other things too numerous to mention." It is claimed that it is made of the purest and most carefully selected herbs which can be obtained. If, however, one picked up two handfuls of dried leaves in the woods and put them in a package, the average man could not distinguish between such rakings and "Dr. D——'s —— Compound" at $1.00 a package.

The *Journal of the American Medical Association* in commenting on this fake, states:

—— Compound is, in short, but one more of the innumerable cure-alls on the market in which discarded, unrecognized or useless drugs are pressed into service and invested with miraculous virtues. What shall be said of men who prey on pregnant women? Who create in the mind of the expectant mother the fear of untold agonies and then offer immunity to these supposititious tortures at the price of their worthless nostrums? Who, with the help of such publications as will accept their lying advertisements, do more to encourage abortion than even the professional abortionists themselves? There seems to be but one remedy: Speed the time when in their acceptance of advertising those publishers who fail to recognize decency as a moral obligation may be forced by public opinion to recognize its value as a business proposition.

[Pg 472]

The C. B. M. Remedy Company: In a small town in Indiana there is a "lady" who has been spending a fortune in giving medical treatment absolutely free to suffering women. The letters, literature, and advertisements by implication lead one to suppose that a woman is in charge of the business of this concern. The advertisements have a picture of a lady giving away packages of medicine. The business was conducted by one F. D. M. The name of his wife was simply used as an advertising asset; the idea, of course, being that a woman would be more willing to write to a business concern telling of her private illnesses if she understood that she was confiding in a woman than she would if under the impression that her letter would be read by a man. This is an old scheme which was employed by others for many years with great success.

M. himself is not a physician and is in no way qualified to give advice to these women who write in response to the advertisements detailing their symptoms and telling of their troubles. Investigation showed that the medicine was compounded by the clerks and stenographers in the employ of the company, and that all communications were answered by form letters. It did not matter what ailed the patient, the treatment was the same.

The claims made by this concern for their remedy, and they had only one, were along the usual line—everything they could think about which has a remote connection with the specialty in which they were interested—leucorrhea, ulceration, displacement or falling of the womb, profuse, scanty or painful periods, uterine or ovarian tumors or growths, and piles from any cause, no matter of how long standing; also pains in the back head and bowels, bearing down feelings, nervousness, creeping feeling up the spine, melancholy, desire to cry, hot flushes, weariness, uterine cancers in their earlier stages.

Analysis of the remedy showed it to be a combination of two weak, commonly used drugs, one a very mild antiseptic and the other a mild astringent. These were held together with cocoa butter into which a drop of carbolic acid may have been put. There is nothing unusual[Pg 473] in the combination, nor has it any wonderful qualities which would justify the claims made in behalf of it. The remedy contains nothing which could under any circumstances effect the removal of cancers, fibroid growths, or polypi, or which is capable of radically relieving laceration of the womb due to child-birth.

The following is one of the specious appeals which this meretricious concern sent to the ailing women of America:

Mrs. M. receives more mail than any other woman in the state.

How would you like to receive so much mail that it would be necessary to use a grindstone in order to open the letters as fast as they come in. This is the way Mrs. C. B. M. opens her mail. She gets tons of mail, and to save time has the letters opened by a large grindstone, which occupies a conspicuous place in her office. No other person in Indiana receives so much mail as she.

Mrs. M.'s aid and advice is as free to you as God's sunshine or the air you breathe. She is always glad to lend her assistance to every suffering woman, and she is a generous, good woman, who has suffered herself as you suffer, and she wants to prove to you that her common sense home treatment will cure you just as surely as it cured her years ago in her humble cottage before riches and fame came to her.

If you are a sufferer from any female trouble, no matter what it is, send the coupon below to Mrs. C. B. M. at once.

I am a woman with all a woman's hopes and fears. I have known what it is to be sick in body and mind. Sick in a way that I couldn't bring myself to explain to a man, even though he were my physician, and I am thankful beyond the power of words to express that I have been given the power to extend to you, my sisters, the priceless boon of relief from the burden of pain and suffering.

I only pray that this little book may be the means of saving some woman from years of such agony as only a woman can know.

I dedicate this book to you.

WOMEN'S DISEASES

I doubt if you can realize the full meaning of these two little words. I, who come in contact with the pitiful wrecks of womanhood wrought by female complaints, know, as I hope you will never know, what shattered lives and broken hearts they cause.

Only a sensitive woman can realize how hard it is to bring[Pg 474] one's self to undergo the ordeal of examination and treatment by a physician.

Every letter sent out by this concern was signed, "Mrs. C. B. M." All literature, every booklet, and every advertisement was ingeniously and seductively "built up" to convey by implication the impression that the business was conducted by a woman, and hence the inference followed in the minds of the simple, trusting victims, that they were writing their secrets, to be read by one of their own sex, and that this woman was professionally qualified and temperamentally capable of giving competent advice and adequate treatment.

Nothing was further from the truth. It was simply a trick, a fraudulent, venal imposition. Mrs. C. B. M. herself admitted that she had absolutely nothing to do with the conduct of the business, nor did her previous experience in any way fit her to give advice in such matters. Her husband established the business under the name of the —— Medicine Company, and continued under this name until after his marriage, when it was reorganized and incorporated in his wife's name. Benefiting by the experience of similar concerns, he then used his wife's name simply as a business asset. How capably and efficiently he utilized this opportunity is shown in the beguiling literature he sent out as the above quotation amply demonstrates.

Think of a man writing, "I am a woman with all a woman's hopes and fears,"—and then proceeding to play, with consummate skill, upon the sensibility and credulity of a sick and neurasthenic woman. It is a round-about way to reach the public pocketbook, but experience has taught these harpies that it is an eminently successful method. Mr. M. himself admitted that the gross receipts from the business were in excess of $100,000 a year, and that 200,000 people were taking treatment from this concern at one time.

Mention has been made of a certain famous compound—which has been characterized by a well-known authority on drug addictions as "a dangerous drug used largely by drinkers." For 23 years after the death of the woman[Pg 475] founder, —— and ——, the owners of the concern, advertised, inviting women to "write to L. P. for advice in regard to their complaints, and being a woman"—though a dead one—"it was easy, for her ailing sisters to pour into her ears every detail of their suffering."

The advertisement as generally printed runs:

No physician in the world has had such a training, or has such an amount of information at hand to assist in the treatment of all kinds of female ills.

This, therefore, is the reason why Mrs. L—— P——, in her laboratory at ——, Mass., is able to do more for the ailing women of America than the family physician. Any woman, therefore, is responsible for her own suffering who will not take the trouble to write to Mrs. P—— for advice.

Does any woman need any further evidence of the fraudulent intent of such concerns? Keep in mind also that this particular remedy is exclusively recommended for "the diseases of women," and contains enough alcohol to render its users victims of the alcoholic habit.

MEDICINE CONCERN RUN BY WOMEN

Dr. D—— runs a mail order business in another town in Indiana. Her specialty is "diseases of women." The business is really owned by W. M. G——, a dealer in teas, coffees, etc. In the advertisements of the concern Dr. D—— emphasizes the fact that she is "a woman—a wife—a mother—a successful physician—a specialist on diseases of women." In many places in the literature of the company the "vast experience" of Dr. D—— is intentionally elaborated.

"Her vast experience as a physician is only one of the qualifications she possesses...."

"Her training and vast experience as a physician enables her to do more for suffering women than any woman can who is not a physician...."

"During several years of active life as a general practitioner she acquired a vast amount of valuable experience that very few ever possess...."

These three quotations emphatically assert that Dr. D. has had "vast" experience "as a general practitioner."[Pg 476] Where did she get this experience as a general practitioner? Inasmuch as she graduated as a physician in 1907 and was licensed to practice in 1908, and as the "—— D—— Company" was chartered in 1908 and began active business then, we ask again, where did she get her "vast experience?"

The following letter, sent by Dr. D—— to one of her prospective patients, gives a general idea of how the "game" is worked. These letters are "form" letters, printed by the thousand, though they are intended to convey the impression that they are personal—the patient's name being inserted. It will be observed that Dr. D——has acquired the specious and oily art of the quack, and the seductive diction of those who live by their wits:

Dear Friend: Since it is your misfortune to be afflicted, I am glad you wrote to me, because I sincerely believe that I can completely cure you if you take my treatment now. Realizing the serious nature of your condition, I at once arranged to give your case my prompt personal attention.

After years of success in curing practically every form of woman's ills, I am devoting my life to my sister women. Being a woman and a mother, I know your every ache and pain and sympathize with you as only a woman can. As a physician, as a specialist in diseases of women I know the causes of your trouble and the most scientific method of curing you quickly. Since you have in me a sympathetic friend as well as a physician I trust you will read carefully my plan for your complete recovery.

A careful diagnosis of your case shows you have Female Weakness.

I have mailed a copy of my book, "Diseases of Women and Home Medical Guide." Be sure to read a description of your condition on pages 25-47.

As requested I have mailed you a free trial of my successful treatment. It is bound to help you and you should take it at once according to my directions enclosed herewith. The free medicines will last you for three days and are suited to your condition, but you should not expect them to cure you. Some of the ingredients contained in the remedies you need are very costly and I cannot afford to give you enough of these medicines to completely cure you.

Your case seems to be of long standing and you really should have a Complete Course of Treatment at once if you are to be completely cured. As I want to do everything possible for you I have prepared a Special Course of Treatment for you and am sending it, postage paid, in the same package with the free remedies.[Pg 477] Please remember that the free remedies are yours to take at once without charge or obligation, but if you use the Special Treatment I shall expect you to send me $3 for it. You need not feel under obligation to me to accept the Special Course, but I know it is just what you need and need NOW, so I feel sure your good judgment will cause you to accept it at your earliest convenience. By sending now I save you some time and ...

Dr. G. M. B., of ——, Mo., advertises to cure deafness, catarrh, asthma and head noises. He offers to send two months' medicine free to prove his ability to cure. In reply to inquiry he practically informs every applicant that his case is so bad that there is no use of sending the two months' treatment. In order to effect a cure in "your case" it is necessary for you to take the regular treatment. He accepts the chance that the literature and the testimonials accompanying his letter will influence the victim to bite. Inasmuch as he admits that his income is about $5,000 per month and that he gets three hundred letters every day, it may be assumed that he knows his business.

It is not necessary to go into details regarding his methods. The following summary of his business was made by the district attorney who investigated it:

I find that the business is being conducted through the post office at ——, Mo., under the names of Dr. —— Remedy Company and Dr. J. M. B——, and is a scheme and device for obtaining money through the mails by means of false and fraudulent pretenses, representations and promises, and I therefore recommend that a fraud order be issued prohibiting the delivery of mail and the payment of money orders to such addresses.

A certain "pure" malt whiskey is advertised as:

"A reliable all-round household remedy."

"It should be in every family medicine chest."

"It is manufactured for the purpose of supplying the profession and public in general with a reliable tonic and stimulant."

"It is a recognized specific to enrich the blood and build body and muscle, and in the prevention and relief of coughs, colds and stomach troubles it has no equal."[Pg 478]

Previous to the passage of the Pure Food and Drug Act it was advertised in the following terms:

BEST SPRING TONIC.

DOCTORS OF ALL SCHOOLS AGREE THAT THE BEST TONIC-STIMULANT TO BUILD UP THE SYSTEM, RUN DOWN AND WEAKENED BY THE LONG STRAIN OF WINTER, AND TO DRIVE OUT SPRING FEVER AND MALARIA IS ——'S MALT WHISKEY.

As a tonic and stimulant it is the greatest strength-giver known to science. It destroys disease germs and by its building and healing properties restores tissues in a gradual, healthy, natural manner. It is a wonderful specific in the treatment and cure of consumption, pneumonia, grippe, bronchitis, coughs, colds, malaria, low fevers, stomach troubles, and all wasting, weakened, diseased conditions, if taken in time.

It is recognized as the world's leading medicine everywhere.

By a decision of the Supreme Court of the State of New York this "pure" malt whiskey has been declared a liquor. It is simply a sweetened whisky. To advertise it as a CURE for consumption or as a cure for any disease was malicious, and should be punishable by a long term in prison. It would be possible to take every statement of the above advertisement and prove each one to be false.

This "pure" malt whiskey is a favorite "booze" of so-called temperance people. Since it is advertised as a medicine, they can get drunk from its use and still be "temperance" advocates. One of the favorite methods of advertising the product was to draw the public's attention to the fact that

CLERGYMEN ENDORSE MALT WHISKY

DISTINGUISHED DIVINES AND TEMPERANCE WORKERS WHO HAVE spent their lives in uplifting their fallen brethren and placing their feet upon the solid rock use and recommend ——'s pure malt whisky. Honored and respected preachers of the gospel and advocates of temperance, without regard to creed or prejudice, make[Pg 479] frank and outspoken statements of what ——'s pure malt whisky has done for them.

Then follow the testimonials and the photographs of three aged and inert-looking preachers.

It made an impressive advertisement, as most nostrum "ads" are, because, unfortunately, the art of the liar is best expressed in the superlative degree. His word-pictures are therefore more lurid, more diversified, more romantic. But when they are investigated and the facts brought to light the advertisement falls to pieces. For example, compare the actual facts relative to the three "distinguished divines" with the fiction in the following advertisement:

The Rev.—— D——, over 82 years of age, practised medicine for many years, when he moved west. He became a minister and did preach for ten years in the State of Wyoming. He then retired from the pulpit and opened a marriage bureau. He received $10.00 when he gave his testimonial "to get his picture taken."

The Rev. —— H—— occupied the pulpit of the Church of Eternal Hope of B——, Pa. He retired to enter politics a number of years ago, and is now a deputy Internal Revenue collector. He is a spiritualist. He owned race horses and was a patron of the turf.

The Rev. McL—— lived in G——, Mich. There are 893 people in the township and it is not even on the railroad line. Mr. McL—— was allowed to resign from the fellowship after being called to trial for endorsing ——'s pure malt whisky.

If these three gentlemen were brought on the stage of any city vaudeville theater and introduced as distinguished divines it would be regarded as a joke—which it really is. If we relegate our "distinguished divines" to marriage bureaus, or the race track, or to the Internal Revenue service, or to preach to flocks in townships of less than one thousand and not on the railroad, the outlook for the ministerial profession is far from encouraging. To tell us that these men spent their lives "in uplifting their fallen brethren" is imposing upon the good nature of one's audience. It is simply one more evidence added to the long list already noted that one does not readily acquire the habit of expecting to read the truth in a patent medicine advertisement. Rather[Pg 480] the reverse. We examine them in expectant curiosity to note their unique and devilish ability to tell picturesque falsehoods.

Certain famous pills are advertised extensively in Great Britain and in the United States. It is claimed by the manufacturers that they are "composed entirely of medicinal herbs" and that they will "cure" constipation, pains in the back, cold chills, bad legs, maladies of indiscretion, kidney and urinary disorders—and several other things.

These pills were analyzed by the British Medical Association's chemists, who reported that they consisted of ginger, soap, and aloes. Where the "medicinal herbs" were it was hard to say.

In large and lurid letters we are informed in the advertisements that these pills are "worth a guinea ($5.00) a box." The retail price is 27 cents a box. The British Medical Association's chemist states that the cost of these pills is one-quarter of a cent per box. Quite a fair margin of profit considering the high cost of living these days!

[Pg 481]

CHAPTER XXXII

THE PATENT MEDICINE EVIL—Continued

Patent Medicine Firms and Quacks Dispose of the Confidential Letters Sent to Them—Patent Medicine Concerns and Letter Brokers—The Patent Medicine Conspiracy Against the Freedom of the Press—How The Patent Medicine Trust Crushes Honest Effort.

HOW QUACKS DISPOSE OF THE CONFIDENTIAL LETTERS SENT TO THEM

When you write for information—which is usually the first step—in reply to an advertisement of this character, you receive in reply a letter, which addresses you in an intimate way, as, "Dear or Esteemed Friend." It informs you that "we are devoting our lives in the interest of suffering humanity," and requests you to waste no time in writing a full account of your symptoms and sickness; that such information will be sacredly regarded as confidential and filed away from the prying eyes of everyone except the "doctor" who reads it.

Every art is used to give the writer the impression that she is doing business with responsible and reputable people; that what she writes about her health, her affairs, and her person, are to be read by an experienced medical adviser and by no other. The truth, as we have shown, is that she writes her secrets to a man, who is not even a physician, who in turn passes the letter over to be answered by an office clerk.

When the fake doctor, or the patent medicine man, has exhausted his "jollying" tactics, his lies, and his promises, and he can no longer induce the victim to send more money, he sells the victim's letters to another quack in the same business. These harpies, knowing what ails the individual, begin sending her their specious and insinuating literature. The woman reads, becomes interested, and, having bitten before, concludes to try[Pg 482] once again, and so the story goes—one after another trying to drain the life-blood of an ailing, irresponsible foolish woman.

The selling of letters has become a business, so much so that there are regularly established medical letter brokers from whom you can buy these letters by the thousands. In a single medical letter broker's office in New York City there are upwards of seven million of these confidential letters for sale to the highest bidders. This incidentally gives one a slight idea of the tremendous business this is, and of the hundreds of thousands of dupes and victims there have been.

The following extracts are taken from a well-known woman's journal, which at various times has been interested in this subject, and are of special interest in this connection:

One of the most disgusting and disgraceful features of the patent medicine business is the marketing of letters sent by patients to patent medicine firms. Correspondence is solicited by these firms under the seal of sacred confidence. When the concern is unable to do further business with a patient it disposes of the patient's correspondence to a letter broker, who, in turn, disposes of it to other patent medicine concerns at the rate of half a cent for each letter.

One of these brokers assured the writer that he could give me "choice lots" of "medical female letters." ... Let me now give you, from the printed lists of these letter brokers, some idea of the way in which these "sacred confidential" letters are hawked about the country. Here are a few samples, all that are really printable:

55,000 "Female Complaint Letters" is the sum total of one item, and the list gives the names of the "medicine company" or the "medical institute" to whom they were addressed. Here is a barter then, in 55,000 letters of a private nature, each one of which, the writer was told, and had a right to expect, would be regarded as "sacredly confidential" by the doctor or concern to whom she had been deluded into telling her private ailments. Yet here they are for half a cent each!

Another batch of some 47,000 letters addressed to five "doctors" and "institutes" is emphasized because they were written by women! A third batch is:

44,000 "Bust Developer Letters,"—letters which one man in a patent medicine concern told me were "the richest sort of reading you could get hold of."

A still further lot offers: 40,000 "Women's Regulator Letters,"—letters[Pg 483] which in their context any woman can naturally imagine would be of the most delicate nature. Still, the fact remains, here they are for sale.

Is not this contemptible?

In the same article is exposed the inhuman greed of patent medicine concerns that turn into cold cash the letters of patients afflicted with the most vital diseases.

To quote again: "All these are made the subject of public barter. Here are offered for sale, for example: 7,000 Paralysis Letters; 9,000 Narcotic Letters; 52,000 Consumption Letters; 3,000 Cancer Letters, and even 65,000 Deaf Letters. Of diseases of the most private nature one is offered here nearly 100,000 letters,—letters the very classification of which makes a sensitive person shudder."

The deeper one delves below the surface of this business the nastier it gets. It is impossible to conceive of vipers and sharks being endowed with more contemptible and brutish qualities than those which characterize the vultures of the patent medicine and quack medical concerns.

THE PATENT MEDICINE CONSPIRACY AGAINST THE FREEDOM OF THE PRESS

It is estimated that the newspapers of the United States get about $100,000,000 per year from the advertisements of patent medicines and fake medical concerns.

There is an association composed of the manufacturers of patent medicines and the owners of advertising medical concerns. It was primarily formed for the single purpose of strictly looking after the "interests" of those concerned.

If we concede, as we must concede if we study the facts, the whole medical advertising business to be disreputable, dishonorable and unjust, in that it is detrimental to the health and welfare of the race, the only protection it could possibly need would be protection against any movement which had for its object the interest of the people who are its victims. This is exactly the key to the workings of the P. A. of America. When one begins to know something about the patent medicine evil, his sense of justice immediately asks why "something"[Pg 484] has not been done to crush it. When the reader understands more about this octopus, he will learn that its tentacles are far-reaching and that it has a mysterious and efficient way of crushing in its incipiency any embryo movement directed against it. It would be a long story to give the facts in detail—they are all a matter of record—the easiest way to explain the procedure is to give an illustration of how the machinery is worked.

Let us suppose a Congressman conceives the idea of introducing a bill in Congress to compel newspapers to refuse advertising matter that is obviously false and that misrepresents facts, and cites, as an example, a patent medicine advertisement. The agent or lobbyist of the association in Washington immediately telegraphs the intent of the bill with the name of its author to the home office of the association. The gentleman in charge of the executive department of the home office looks up the facts regarding the political connections of the Congressman, wires to the papers published in his district suggesting to them the advisability of using their influence to change the Congressman's opinion. The newspapers do as they are bid (though there are a few who have refused to do this kind of work, but only a few); they may intimate to him that he is committing political suicide, or they may adopt other tactics. The result, however, is that the representative usually sees the point and permits his bill to die in committee. The quacks are not satisfied with this single effort to ensure the death of the bill. The matter is taken up with other Congressmen through their home papers; the whole machinery of the system is set in motion. Their attention is called to the bill. They are told that the public does not demand such legislation, and that, if this bill passes, it will deprive of many thousands of dollars for advertising the papers which are friendly toward the political future of the particular Congressman in question. The facts are thus brought to the attention of many Congressmen. They see the point also. It suggests to them that they will do well not to trample on this monster or they may suffer themselves. Thus are the people deprived of what might have been a great step forward[Pg 485] in the fight for pure food and drugs and, incidentally, in the preservation of the public health.

One may pertinently ask why the newspapers lend themselves to such infamous and dishonorable dealings. The answer is that, inasmuch as they derive a very large part of their total income from patent medicine advertisements and as these advertisements are contracted for under certain conditions, it can readily be seen that they are made a party to crushing legislation which would interfere with the patent medicine business.

It is agreed in case any law or laws are enacted, either State or national, harmful to the interest of the —— Company, that this contract may be cancelled by them from date of such enactment, and the insertions made paid for pro rata with the contract price.

There is another feature of the contract that is of the utmost significance and importance to the mothers of the race. It is the only instance we know of which effectually muzzles the public press. This part of the contract reads as follows:

It is agreed that the —— Company may cancel this contract,... in case any matter otherwise detrimental to the —— Company's interest is permitted to appear in the reading columns or elsewhere in the paper.

This means that the newspapers bind themselves, under contract, not to print any matter in their reading columns which would be detrimental to the interests of the patent medicine manufacturers. Under the same stipulation they cannot even accept matter to be paid for, if it in any way reflects upon the patent medicine business. In other words, the sovereign people, whose servant the public press should be, is, under this contract, deprived of its rights of representation in the columns of the daily newspapers.

The grave significance of this condition of affairs will be adequately appreciated when it is remembered that every popular movement to right public wrongs must have the fullest publicity or the effort is doomed to failure. The patent medicine business has been shown to[Pg 486] be a monstrously evil institution, yet every effort to enlist the public press in an effort to arouse the necessary degree of indignation which precedes every public demand for the righting of a wrong has failed, because, "it is agreed that the —— Company may cancel this contract in case any matter otherwise detrimental to the —— Company's interest is permitted to appear in the reading columns or elsewhere in the paper."

There is another feature of this ugly business which is of the deepest interest to women. The patent medicine territory is the whole country. It is a large, profitable field. A movement was once started by certain reputable New York physicians, who were deeply interested in this question, to discover a means to aid the class who buy patent medicines and support the fake medical concerns. It was thought that if an advertising propaganda was instituted, offering to give legitimate and adequate medical advice, at the lowest possible cost, there would be many who would avail themselves of the opportunity. The following advertisement was prepared and given out for publication, with the result that it could not be advantageously placed:

RELIABLE MEDICAL ADVICE.

Government investigation of the PATENT MEDICINE BUSINESS and of the advertised MEDICAL CURE CONCERNS, has demonstrated that they are worthless and dangerous; that they are money making schemes only, and that they acquire business by misrepresentation, by falsehood, and by fraudulent testimonials. Most of these concerns are owned by men with no medical education or experience.

These are facts attested to by the highest authorities in the United States, and apply to every advertised remedy and to every system of advertised treatment in the newspapers to-day with no exception that has come to our knowledge.

A BUREAU OF PHYSICIANS, each in good standing and in active private practice, has been established in NEW YORK CITY, to extend advice to those requiring medical assistance.

The object of the bureau is to prevent patients from placing themselves in the hands of incompetent, expensive and fraudulent schemers. The character of the advice furnished[Pg 487] will be exactly the same as if you visited the office of any up-to-date reputable city consultant. We will simply direct what should be done in each instance to effect relief of the diseased conditions.

The charges will be the ordinary fees charged by reputable physicians anywhere for similar services, and will in no instance be unreasonable or excessive.

We invite the correspondence of those in need of honest advice. Ask for information which will be sent free of charge.

Here was a tremendously lucrative field in which there was every possibility of doing a large amount of genuine good, which, however, could not be reached by men whose only object was to benefit the people, because the public press did not dare publish anything detrimental to "the combine." If this isn't monopoly, what is it?

This is not the only instance of this kind that has taken place. One independently wealthy gentleman, for certain business reasons of his own, conceived the idea of inserting a trustworthy article exposing the patent medicine combine in the newspapers of the country, for which he was, of course, willing to pay the usual advertising rates. He gave the contract to a large advertising concern which began the crusade in Texas, the *intention* being to cover the country working the States one after the other. What was the result? As soon as the system's attention was directed to the plan the mandate of "silence" was flashed to the newspapers and the propaganda died an unnatural death in Texas, whose borders it never crossed. The columns of the public press were tightly closed to it.

Is it any wonder that it has been so difficult to pass a Public Health bill? I am hopeful, however, that the women will solve this problem. It would seem to be a subject in which they could become strenuously and eagerly interested. Women as voting factors, or as legislators, will never succeed in the subtle fights of ward politics, or in the coarser slugging battles of graft and patronage, but in the moral finesse, necessary to achieve success in public health and purity legislation they should prove to be enthusiasts. If the regeneration of the race[Pg 488] is entangled in legislative procedure or political subtilties, its only salvation is to find emancipators whose heart strings are of finer and truer fiber than those in the breasts of men. We hope to find them in the mothers of the race.

[Pg 489]

CHAPTER XXXIII

THE PATENT MEDICINE EVIL—Continued

The Patent Medicine Evil and the Duty of the Mothers of the Race—"Blood-Money"—The People Must be the Reformers—Mothers' Resolutions.

THE PATENT MEDICINE EVIL AND THE DUTY OF THE MOTHERS OF THE RACE

It may be emphatically asserted that the patent medicine evil and the fraudulent medical cure more directly concern the mothers of the race than any others. No matter who the ailing victim may be, some woman is deeply and sincerely interested in his, or her, recovery and welfare. If the proper influence is exerted at the right time, and if it is based upon adequate knowledge of the danger involved, it is certain that the sufferer will not become a victim of the fraudulent and dangerous advertised nostrum, or a fake medical course of treatment. If each mother, therefore, possessed an adequate knowledge of the patent medicine evil, and exerted the influence which would naturally result from the possession of such knowledge, we should soon see the end of the whole business.

Most people are honest and sincere. It is difficult, however, to arouse the majority to concerted and sustained action. If the honest and well-intentioned element in society could be influenced to a sustained effort to correct existing evils, in any department of human effort, the fraudulent and dishonest members of society could be effectually rendered harmless. If the suggestion which I have advanced in the article on Eugenics, to form Eugenic Clubs in every community, should be adopted, the members could, in a definite way, contribute to the propaganda, by insisting that the members of the legislature and Congress inform themselves upon these subjects, and act and vote in accordance with the sentiment of their constituents. It is only by some such systematized, concerted[Pg 490] effort that any hope may be reasonably entertained that this question will be satisfactorily and finally solved. That it is capable of being solved satisfactorily there is no doubt whatever. It depends upon the women.

The passage of The Pure Food and Drugs Act, caused, for a brief period, a cessation of the strenuous activity which had previously characterized the patent medicine business. It was not, however, to be expected that any single legislative act would permanently strangle such a parasite,—for we must remember that it is an easy and a highly remunerative calling. Nor was it to be expected that men who are adepts in sophistry and experts in quibbling could not find a way to circumvent the intent of the law.

This was proved to be so because they are again beginning to advertise more freely and with more assurance. One of the best known has assumed a new advertising garb. Its new diction is specious and clever, but it is a satanic cleverness when its history is weighed in the balance. It is quite probable that its formula may have been slightly changed, but at the end of each advertisement the following suggestive paragraph appears:

"SPECIAL NOTICE—Many persons are making inquiries for the old-time ——. To such would say, that this formula is now put out under the name of ——, manufactured by —— Company, C——, Ohio. Write them and they will be pleased to send you a free booklet."

The old time —— was condemned by the United States Government as an intoxicant and stimulant, and cures were sold in various parts of the country for the —— "jag," yet in the new advertisement the following appears:

"—— is a remedy that should be kept in the house. Its virtue as a preventive to disease is the thing I wish chiefly to emphasize.

"When once the value of —— as a household remedy is understood no home would be without it. Cathartics, pills and powders would be discarded. Irritating tonics would be no longer taken. ALCOHOLIC DRINKS WOULD HAVE NO PLACE...."

If "alcoholic drinks would have no place" in the household,[Pg 491] why should one want this "remedy," which has no medical value except as a stimulant? It is as if a drunken man should deliver a temperance lecture: it would really be funny if we did not know the tragedies that have gone before as a result of its use. That is an example of the type of argument which must be legislated against.

There are two specific points in this crusade against the patent medicine fraud which should be the objective issues of all concerted effort to crush the evil. These could be taken up by mothers in their eugenic clubs and developed until successfully legislated upon. It would be the greatest immediate contribution to constructive legislation that women's suffrage could bestow upon the race.

First, to enact a law which would make it a felony for a newspaper to print a fraudulent patent medicine advertisement, or a fake medical cure. A national board of competent authority should be constituted to determine the question of fraud.

Second, to amend the law which permits the registration of a fancy name for a combination of drugs, without at the same time giving the formula.

The mothers of the race must recognize that it is not only a question of economy, but a vital issue in health preservation, to regard all advertised remedies and medical "cures" as absolutely dangerous and worthless, and consequently not to be used at all. There is no safe exception to this rule. The records teem with evidence condemning the whole discreditable business. Almost without exception, every advertised remedy and cure has been, when actually investigated, found fraudulent and worthless. The great majority of these concerns are owned and run by individuals, who have had no medical experience, and no training to fit them to advise patients in any sense. It is a money-making scheme pure and simple, and anyone who asks further proof is not open to conviction.

I believe the truthful and the just interpretation of the success of the patent medicine business is to be found in the ignorance of the people,—not the kind of ignorance that reflects upon their intelligence, but real, honest ignorance regarding the true character and merit of the patent[Pg 492] medicine business. It would be an unwarranted reflection upon the intelligence and acumen of the American people to assert that they would wittingly support a fraudulent proposition, especially a proposition whose success meant their own physical degeneration. The reflection is rather an indictment of the inefficiency of those in authority.

We must not deny that there exists in the minds of the lowly a feeling that what is printed is true. This is as it should be; it is an instinct and it is fundamental. We must remember, too, that there are thousands and thousands of homes, into which absolutely no literature of any kind ever penetrates except the weekly, and it may be stray copies of the daily newspaper. These people are primitive and credulous. They have ailing members in the family, and they have not always accessible medical service, or they may be too poor to avail themselves of such service as exists. When, therefore, they see glaring promises of relief and "cures" for whatever may ail them, in the oft-read paper, week after week, it is an easy step to become enrolled as a victim. These people believe in their newspaper. They have no reason to question the truth of its contents. They unconsciously put their trust and dependence upon those in authority, those who should see to it that the instinct of truth and honesty is reflected in the justice and protection which is meted out to the helpless and the poor. Is it any wonder, therefore, that we have victims, when the only voice that comes to them from the great world beyond is a tissue of false promises and fraudulent pretensions? The law is a cumbersome vehicle to move. It cannot be driven by inspiration—no matter how crucial the incentive may be that creates the inspiration,—it moves only by the potential force of a great conviction, the voice of the people. It seems a pity to waste time in the education of all the people before their voice shall be raised to demand protection, when the authorities know now of the wrong that is being perpetrated and could right it without the waste of this precious time.

Since we cannot hope for legislative assistance until the people are aroused to demand it, every mother who has an opportunity to learn the truth about the matter,[Pg 493] must become a member of the propaganda of education and must spread the knowledge to others. We must educate the army of innocents who fall because they do not know the truth, and we must reach that vaster army, whose gullibility permits these frauds to flourish. We must show them the false foundation and the hollow pretense upon which such schemes are founded. We must show them that each detail of the business is inspired by a wrong motive; that the so-called personal letters even are printed by the hundreds of thousands, and filled in to appear as personal communications by office clerks who possess absolutely no medical knowledge; that the "diagnosis" blanks are worthless and frequently dangerous, and simply sent to the prospective victim to impress him and draw him on; that the medicine furnished, is, as a rule, made of the cheapest of drugs, bought in large quantities from parties, whose reputation in the drug trade is not of the best; that the medicine has no special potency nor value, that it is in all likelihood a worthless mixture, which in the advertisements is given false and lying properties; that when they have got all the money out of the victim possible they will sell his letters to other nostrum venders. It is a sorry reflection on our civilization that the sick, often the incurably ill, cannot be protected against their own credulity and the devices of those who would fatten on their misfortune and profit by their sufferings.

If every mother who reads this article would quietly think the matter over and reach a definite conclusion as to just how she may contribute her share to the educational crusade to crush the patent medicine monster, I am certain it would not be long before we would begin to feel that there were the "mutterings of a storm brewing." If each mother would subscribe to the following resolution, and obey it, she would really be an agency for much good in her community:

I resolve never to advise an ailing friend or acquaintance to purchase or use an advertised remedy or "cure" of any kind whatsoever; nor will I permit any other person to advise the use of such remedies or "cures" without, in a friendly way, protesting, and thereby converting this person, who undoubtedly is ignorant of the facts.[Pg 494]

I further resolve, always to advise an ailing friend to consult someone, whose education and experience qualifies him to give competent advice.

I would suggest that the above resolution be printed on cards in the form of a motto, to be hung on the wall, and distributed from house to house by the eugenic clubs. At the bottom of the card, the word "over" should be clearly printed. On the reverse side, in ordinary reading type should be a condensed and efficient argument against the use of patent medicines. This argument should be complete and convincing in itself, so that one who may casually ask what the card means may be told to read what is on the back of the card, and may, thereby, be convinced that "it is a good idea." This would be an inexpensive way of exciting the curiosity of the community, and when the psychological moment arrives it would probably be possible for one of the members of the club to give an address or lecture on the patent medicine evil. Inasmuch as the curiosity and the sympathy of the audience would be with the speaker, it would only be necessary to state facts to make converts. It seems worth trying, and the suggestion is given with the hope that the women in every community who are capable (and there are capable leaders in every community) will take this club idea up and develop it far beyond the largest hopes which I conceive for them.

If eugenics means anything, and if the women are what they claim, much will be accomplished by each doing her part intelligently, and by each community standing upon its own record.